Publisher
buybook
Radićeva 4, Sarajevo
Telephone:+387 33 716-450, 716-451
Zelenih beretki 8, Sarajevo
            +387 33 712-010, 712-011
E-mail: fabrikaknjiga@buybook.ba
              www.buybook.ba

For Publisher
Goran Samardžić
Damir Uzunović

Authors
Tim Clancy
Willem van Eekelen

Contributing author
John Snyder

Design
Nedim Meco

Printed in Croatia by Zrinski

CIP - Katalogizacija u publikaciji
Nacionalna i univerzitetska biblioteka
Bosne i Hercegovine, Sarajevo

338.483 (497.6) (036)

CLANCY, Tim
    Herzegovina : a guided journey through
Herzegovina / Tim Clancy, Willem van Eekelen. -
Sarajevo : Buybook, 2005. - 164 str. : ilustr. ;
22 cm

ISBN 9958-630-62-0
1. Eekelen, Willem van
COBISS.BH-ID 13953798

A GUIDED JOURNEY THROUGH

HERZEGOVINA

Tim Clancy
Willem van Eekelen

buybook
Sarajevo, 2006

A guide to Herzegovina

I fondly dedicate this book of my favourite region in BiH to my
favourite people in the world.
**Thanks mom, dad, Dan, Nan and
my wonderful sister Jenny.**

**In loving memory of Imtias Stranjak
rest in peace my dear friend.**

THE SERIES

As Bosnia and Herzegovina emerges as one of the newest and most exciting tourist destinations in Europe, there is a growing need for detailed and thorough information on this country. In response to this demand **buybook** publishing company now offers a series of new books that cover the cultural, historical, natural and culinary heritage of Bosnia and Herzegovina. Four books are on the shelves already:

- Sarajevo and the surrounding areas
- Herzegovina
- Central and North Bosnia
- Forgotten Beauty – Hiking to BiH's highest peaks

More titles are to follow.

The first part of the regional guides is a general introduction to Bosnia and Herzegovina. This section is the same for each of the guides and provides you with the standard information needed to enjoy a journey in any part of the country. The second part of each guide is a comprehensive and region-specific travel companion, covering hotels, restaurants, café's and clubs, transport, travel agencies and a wide range of activities for all types of visitor. Each guide also has an eco-tourism section highlighting the natural beauties, flora and fauna, wildlife photography, fly-fishing, and more. The guides cover all major destinations, but also a great many places that are off the beaten track. In many cases, you will need a detailed map to find these hidden treasures.

Welcome to the brighter side of Bosnia and Herzegovina – enjoy your trip!!

CONTENTS

ACKNOWLEDGEMENTS

We're happy to say that there are many people to thank. Where to start? Let's go full circle... this project started in 2001, during our hike in one of Europe's last primeval forests in Sutjeska National Park. Two things struck us: this was the most beautiful place we had ever seen, and there wasn't a soul in sight. Tourists, apparently, didn't know about this country's beauty.

Three years later, in the spring of 2004, Paddy Ashdown and three representatives from Bosnia and Herzegovina traveled around Europe to shed some light on this hidden little treasure called Bosnia and Herzegovina. This generated, perhaps for the first time, large scale interest in the 'lighter side' of this country. To turn interest into visits, people need information – henceforth, our chance to write this booklet!

The creation of this series had many contributors. The Japan International Cooperation Agency allowed us to use their wonderful research, which greatly enhanced the eco-tourism section of this series. John Snyder did some of the best research on wildlife habitats, fly-fishing, fish species identification and the entire eco-tourism package to date. The European Youth Group, with its great corps of volunteers, did great research on Sarajevo and Banja Luka. Boris Rebac, Barbara-Anne Krijgsman and many people at the various tourism associations suggested valuable additions. Jim Marshall did many fine-tunings to the text and his tremendous knowledge of the conflict will certainly help the reader understand a bit better what happened here. Others wrote texts as well – as is indicated in the text. Thanks to Trudi Bolten and Hans van Eekelen too: they edited the first part of this booklet.

Azra Skajlo at Green Visions showed once again how patient she can be after we repeatedly placed tasks on her desk to check and double-check phone numbers, addresses and whatever else was needed. Thanks Azra. The same thanks go to Suad Salkić, who spent many evenings verifying and adding all sorts of things.

Brank Media were very generous and allowed us to use some of their amazing photographs. The Dutch Embassy kindly covered much of the costs of producing this series. For that to happen, Hans de Vries did his bit of proposal writing – and came to love the country so much that he is now married to Sabina. Thanks Hans, and congratulations!

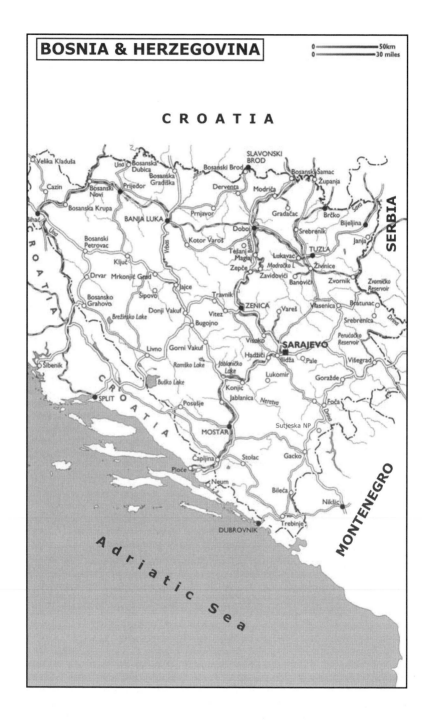

Part one: THE COUNTRY

BACKGROUND INFORMATION

Facts & Figures

Location: Southeast Europe, bordering Croatia (932 km), Serbia (312 km) and Montenegro (215 km)

Land area: 51,129 km^2

Status: Republic

Languages: Bosnian, Croatian, Serbian

Population: probably around 3.8 million

Religions: Muslim (44%), Orthodox Christian (32%), Roman Christian (17%), Others (7%)

Capital: Sarajevo, with a population of around 400,000

Other major cities and towns in the country: Banja Luka, Tuzla, Zenica, Mostar, Bihać

Administrative division: The country is divided into two entities: the Federation of Bosnia and Herzegovina, and the Republika Srpska. The Federation of Bosnia and Herzegovina is subdivided into ten cantons.

Time: CET (GMT + 1 hour)

Currency: Convertible Mark (KM or BAM)

International telephone code: +387

Bosnia and Herzegovina is a long name for a country that measures just over 50,000 km^2. Bosnia covers the north and centre of the country. Its name is probably derived from 'bosana', an old Indo-European word meaning water, and refers to the country's many rivers, streams and springs. The southern region of ancient Hum, ruled by Herceg Stjepan (Duke Stjepan), was later named Herzegovina after the region was conquered by the invading Ottomans. Together, these two areas form a triangular country in the middle of what used to be Yugoslavia. It is a mountainous country that borders on Croatia and Serbia & Montenegro, two other former Yugoslav republics. It is here that eastern and western civilizations met, often clashed but also enriched and reinforced each other.

GEOGRAPHY

The trip from Sarajevo to Mostar is a two-hour drive. Halfway, a tunnel links Bosnia to Herzegovina. On the one side of this tunnel there is lush vegetation on gently rolling hills. On the other side there are the high, rugged mountains of the Dinaric Alps. This mountain range is the natural boundary of the Mediterranean and continental Alpine climates. The warm Adriatic temperatures clash with the harsher Alpine ones, producing one of the most diverse eco-systems in Europe. A bit further towards Mostar, these mountains are gone again and you are in a fertile flatland. That is Bosnia and Herzegovina: three worlds in a two hour drive. Had I been in a different bus when writing this section, I would have started it with moonlands, waterfalls, piping hot spring water steaming up to the road, snow (in May), fierce rivers, thick medieval forests and green mountain lakes.

Land

Much of Bosnia and Herzegovina is mountainous. The long chain of the Southern Alps – the Dinaric Alps - stretches from northwest Croatia through the heart of Bosnia and Herzegovina and into Montenegro, and finishes in the Prokletija Mountains on the Albanian border. Herzegovina hosts the highest and wildest of this mountain range, which for centuries provided the population protection from Roman invaders, and which slowed the Ottoman conquest of Bosnia.

Other parts of the country – even the other mountainous parts - look very different from the rugged Alpines. The central belt of Bosnia has both rocky mountains and green, rolling hills covered with conifer forests and lined with countless freshwater streams and rivers. Some northern areas are part of the long and agriculturally rich plains that extend from Hungary, through Slavonia and Croatia into the fertile fields of the Sava and Drina River valleys. Part of the northwest of the country is all karst topography, with deep limestone caves and underground rivers. These limestone fields are connected to the low limestone valleys of the south. Together, they form the single largest karst field in the world.

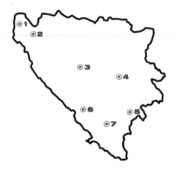

Waterfalls

1. Bukovi na Uni ili Veliki slap
2. Štrbački buk
3. Vodopad Plive
4. Vodopad Skakavac
5. Vodopad Skakavci
6. Kravice
7. Provalija

Mountains

1. Maglić, 2396m
2. Volujak, 2336m
3. Velika Ljubušnja, 2238m
4. Čvrsnica, 2226m
5. Vranica, 2110m
6. Prenj, 2103m
7. Treskavica, 2086m
8. Vran, 2074m
9. Bjelašnica, 2067m
10. Lelija, 2032m
11. Zelengora, 2014m
12. Cincar, 2006m

Mountains in Bosnia and Herzegovina

The Dinaric mountains

From the high central ranges, the Dinaric Alps cut east towards Visočica, Bjelašnica, and Treskavica Mountains. This area has some very deep canyons. Many of the highland settlements here date back to medieval times. Moving further east, bordering Montenegro, are Bosnia and Herzegovina's highest peaks. Protected in Sutjeska National Park, Maglić Mountain (2,386m) towers above the surrounding natural fortresses of Zelengora Mountain, Volujak, Lelija and the Mesozoic walls of Lebršnik Mountain. The young limestone mountains of the Dinaric system can be found in the middle part of the county. Together, these three sub-areas are good for ten peaks above the 2000 metre mark.

Vran	2074m
Čvrsnica	2226m
Čabulja	1789m
Velež	1969m
Prenj	2103m
Bjelašnica	2067m
Visočica	1974m
Crvanj	1921m
Treskavica	2086m
Lelija	2032m
Zelengora	2014m
Ljubišna	2242m
Volujak	2336m
Maglić	2396m (highest peak in the country)

Then, there is the mountain range that forms the natural connection between Herzegovina and Bosnia.

Ivan	950m
Makljen	1123m
Kupreška vrata	1324m
Čemerno	1293m

And lastly, to the north, next to the river Sava and the low basin of the Bosna River, lies the flat valley of Posavina, surrounded by a long stretch of low mountains. These mountains are not high, but they are impressive as they rise like lonely islands out of the valley.

Majevica	916m
Motajnica	652m
Vučjak	368m
Prosara	363m
Kozara	977m

Water

Bosnia and Herzegovina is a country full of water. Much of that water flows under the ground. You can hear it, but you can't always see it. Some underground water exits in the form of submarine springs in the Adriatic Sea. Other water gushes from mountain sides, in springs that come hot and cold and in all shapes and intensities. Many springs appear as a gentle stream, but in Blagaj it's a whole river that gushes out of the mountain. Most water is crystal clear, but some water carries such a density of minerals that the water is colored.

Some water feeds into lakes. The Deransko-Svitavsko Lakes are part of Hutovo blato, a large bird reserve in the south of the country. Boračko Lake and Blidinje Lake are equally beautiful and maintain their own eco-systems. Perhaps even more spectacular are the glacial lakes in the mountain regions of Prenj, Čvrsnica, Satora, Vranica, Treskavica, Crvanj and Volujak.

The country's biggest lake - Buško Lake – is manmade. With an average size of 55km^2, this lake was formed by regulating the waters of the Livanjsko and Duvanjsko valleys, destroying, as artificial lakes often do, unique eco-systems in the process. The most popular tourist lakes are artificial as well: the lakes of Jablanica and Modrac, both formed by hydroelectric dams.

CLIMATE

In Bosnia and Herzegovina, Mediterranean and Alpine influences meet and create a mosaic of climate types within a relatively small area. The south enjoys warm, sunny and dry weather, with very mild winters. In the more continental areas the weather is similar to that of central Europe – hot summers, cool springs and autumns, and cold winters with considerable snowfall. The Mediterranean and continental climates meet in the middle, creating eco-systems that cannot be found anywhere else.

The mountains create a climate of their own. The Alpine climate rules the mountain terrains of the high Dinarics above 1700 meters. The winters there are extremely cold, with temperatures well below zero for more than six months of the year. Snow covers the terrain until summer and the winds often reach hurricane strength.

FLORA AND FAUNA

Bosnia and Herzegovina faces the challenge of preserving its natural wealth, and it is not well prepared. Less than one percent of Bosnia and Herzegovina's land surface is protected – compared to the European average of seven percent – and the country risks losing much of its pristine wilderness and forests to uncontrolled development, clear cutting, and exploitation of its abundant fresh water supply.

Flora

Beech, oak, evergreen, chestnut, spruce and dozens of other types of trees form thick forests that cover over a third of the country. Conversely, black pines often stand alone. Shaped like skinny mushrooms, they do not require earth and grow on rocks, sometimes all alone on otherwise barren mountainsides.

Many of the country's forests are absolutely spectacular, but none matches the rough beauty of Perućica forest. This primeval forest dates back over 20,000 years. It lays in a valley, hidden below Maglić Mountain, the country's highest peak. Here, massive beech trees are complemented by the high black pines that grow on the rock faces that surround the valley. A hike through the heart of these woodlands is an unforgettable and awe-inspiring experience.

The climates suit a surprising variety of plants and trees. The country's central and eastern forests are very similar to those found in northern and central Europe. Herzegovina and western Bosnia, which are covered by large areas of karst, are characterized by vegetation typical of the coastal and mountainous regions of the Mediterranean.

Unsurprisingly, the country's two large floral regions intersect along the same lines, and have a richness that only tropical and sub-tropical regions can match. Very favorable conditions have preserved species from the times of diluvia glaciations right up to the present. Together, the Euro-Siberian and Mediterranean floral regions are home to over 3,700 species of flowering plants, including hundreds of endemic species (species that are unique to the region). If you like flowers, come in spring. You will see them, in their thousands, in all shapes, sizes and colors, and absolutely everywhere.

Fauna

Bosnia and Herzegovina was once home to one of the largest bear popula-tions in the world and had thriving wolf, deer, wild boar and wild goat communities. These populations suffered severely from the war. Through-out the conflict many frontlines were in the high mountain regions. This exposed bear, wild goat, wild boar and wolf populations to heavy gun and artillery fire, and to being hunted for food by soldiers. Many have been killed, or fled to quieter forests in neighboring countries.

Despite their diminished numbers it is not uncommon to see a bear, or occasionally a wolf, in Sutjeska National Park in eastern Bosnia. Most wild goats live in Herzegovina's Neretva Valley, but some are found in Sutjeska National Park and on the southern slopes of Bjelašnica and Visočica Mountains as well. Wild boars have even made a real comeback and are experiencing population overgrowth. They are usually found in lush, coni-fer areas in the medium sized mountain ranges but can be occasionally be spotted in Herzegovina as well. In addition, there are foxes, otters, pine martens, bobcats, deer, porcupines, many types of snakes and a variety of other little creatures in the country's large stretches of untouched wilder-ness.

There is a plethora of birds as well. Hutovo blato is the largest bird migration centre in southeast Europe. In these marshy wetlands in south-ern Herzegovina you can find 240 types of birds, many of them on a migra-tion path between Europe and North Africa. Heron, Greek partridge, coot, owls, pheasants, and wild duck permanently make their home in this tiny oasis. The Brdača Reserve in the north of the country is also a haven for many types of birds and is in the process of attaining protection status. But you don't have to come to parks to see rare birds. The high mountains have always been home to eagles, hawks and falcons and it is not uncom-mon to see them on a walk or hike almost anywhere in the country. Driving on the main highway from Bihać towards Bosanski Petrovac you are almost guaranteed to spot large hawks perched on the old electricity cables lining the road.

Illegal hunting

In talks about the tourism potential of Bosnia and Herzegovina, people in the business regularly list their hunting grounds as attraction number one. Hunters should come to Bosnia and Herzegovina, they say, and shoot bear. This is illegal, but appar-ently hunting regulation is so poorly enforced that some people feel they can ignore it completely. That is most unfortunate, as bear and other populations have been depleted as a consequence of illegal hunting, mines, and a mass exodus during the war years.

Fish are abundant in Bosnia and Herzegovina. Most of the fresh water rivers are teeming with trout. Carp, grayling, and bass are found through-out the country. These fish are of some economic importance: the first organized tour group that returned to Bosnia and Herzegovina after the war was here for fly-fishing, and this type of tourism is bound to increase, creating employment in otherwise rather peripheral parts of the country.

PEOPLE

The geography and climate of Bosnia and Herzegovina have had a profound influence on the country's people. A rugged and creative mountain culture has emerged from this region, connecting man and nature in ways rarely seen in modern times. Every second mountain walk will pass by an ancient village that preserves 'old world' Europe. Here, modern medicines and exotic spices will never replace the medicinal herbs that have long been used to cure illnesses, heal wounds, improve circulation and spice up meals.

In the open valleys between these mountains sprawl Mostar, Jablanica, Konjic, Sarajevo, Foča and many other towns. They are all very old. Some of them – Mostar, Travnik – once grew at strategic places along trade routes. Others – Srebrenica, Tuzla – were founded on the wealth of minerals. Gold, silver, salt, and copper have all been mined here since Roman times.

In the south, the rivers and Mediterranean climate offer ideal conditions for agricultural settlements, and the Neretva River Valley and the Neretva Delta have been inhabited since the Paleolithic Age. These areas produce fruits such as figs, oranges, mandarins, and pomegranates, and have had a winemaking tradition since Roman times. In the north, water has been equally valuable. Jointly, the Una, Sana and Vrbas Rivers have long protected the area against invaders. The fertile valleys these rivers created are sacred to their inhabitants, and guests will find these rivers spoken of as members of the family.

DEMOGRAPHICS

According to the last population census there were 4,354,911 inhabitants in Bosnia and Herzegovina in 1991. Due to war-related death and migration, that number is lower now. Policy makers estimate that the country's population is now around 3.8 million people and steadily growing, and that over one million Bosnians now live abroad. The ethnic composition remains similar to the pre-war percentages: Bosniacs (Muslims) 44%, Serbs (Christian Orthodox) 32%, and Croats (Catholics) 17%. The remaining 7% of the population is composed of Yugoslavs, Albanians, Gypsies, Jews, and several other minority groups.

If ever a new census were to be held, I would be intrigued to know the population's division by sex. Wherever I look, I see more women than men. Is that true, or could it be my flawed perspective? The war probably had its impact. But isn't the male-dominated fighting compensated by the female-dominated outward migration? I don't know. A few friends told me that women have always outnumbered men in some of the country's main towns and cities.

LANGUAGE

The politics of language

Americans speak English; Austrians speak German; and until not long ago the southern Slavs spoke Serbo-Croatian. The political fractions that occurred in the early 1990's brought along with it the politics of language as well. Bosnian, Croatian and Serbian barely differ at all, but are nonetheless considered three different languages. It is a political choice, not a linguistic reality, as the border police illustrated when I said the exact same sentence four times when driving from Sarajevo to Belgrade via Croatia:

Exiting Bosnia and Herzegovina: 'Hey, where did you learn to speak Bosnian?'

Entering Croatia: 'Hey, where did you learn to speak Croatian?'

Exiting Croatia: 'Hey, where did you learn to speak Croatian?'

Entering Serbia and Montenegro: 'Hey, where did you learn to speak Serbian?'

The pre-war language of former Yugoslavia was Serbo-Croat. This term is virtually extinct now. Nowadays, there are three 'official' languages spoken in Bosnia and Herzegovina: Bosnian, Croatian, and Serbian. Local people attach great importance to the name of the language. For practical purposes, these languages are one and the same. The differences are similar to those between American and British English.

Bosnian/Croatian/Serbian is a Slavic language. Many words are similar in Czech or Slovakian, even Polish and Ukrainian. The language is distinctly different from but part of the same family as Russian. Illustrating the common Ottoman past, there are many Ottoman words that Bosnia and Herzegovina shares with the Egyptian dialect of Arabic.

In the Federation only the Latin alphabet is used, but in the Republika Srpska, the other of the two entities of Bosnia and Herzegovina, many signs are in Cyrillic. This includes road signs. If you are unable to decipher that script you might find it difficult to know exactly where you are.

In the cities it is not uncommon to find English-speaking people. Because of the large refugee and migrant population that lived in Germany during the war there are many German speakers as well. In the rural areas neither language is spoken among the adults, but there may well be children able to chat with you in English. Some useful words and phrases can be found in the language section of the Appendix.

Sign Language

Although isolated by a large mountain range, Bosnia and Herzegovina possesses many Mediterranean characteristics. Body and hand language is one of them. If a non-English speaking person is having trouble communicating with you, be prepared for him or her using other means to get the message across. People here don't behave like British or Americans and just speak louder – they *move*. So:

- If a Bosnian makes a waving motion (sort of like 'come here') in the vicinity of his or her mouth: would you like to eat?

- If a local takes a hitchhiker's thumb and bobs it towards his or her mouth: would you like a drink?

- If one pinches the forefinger and thumb together, with the pinky finger out and gently bobs the hand: let's go for a coffee.

- If the right arm shoots up above the shoulder: either 'forget it' or 'screw you'…your call.

- If the right arm sweeps across the front of the chest like hitting a ball or something: 'don't worry about it'…'so what'

- A thumbs up does not mean you are great or that things are OK – it means one, the number one.

- The neck disappearing into the shoulders and both hands shrugging in front means 'it wasn't me' or 'how do I know?'

- The index and pointer finger, tapped against the lips: can you spare a cigarette?

ECONOMY

Imagine this. There is a place that goes through a devastating war. Before the war, the place was a relatively poor and underdeveloped part of a country with a centrally planned economy. After the war, the place is an independent nation in the midst of an intensely competitive free market world economy. Before the war, there used to be import protection and there were secure trade links with the wealthier republics of the country it then belonged to. In times of hardship, these wealthier republics cushioned the blows by providing some economic support. After the war, this now independent nation is bound by free trade agreements with the rest of the world. Even without any further impediments, businesses would find it almost impossible to compete successfully in this whole new setting. This place, obviously, is Bosnia and Herzegovina, and unfortunately there *are* further impediments.

Before the war, Bosnia and Herzegovina concentrated on the production of basic goods (wood, agricultural produce, iron bars) and intermediate products (parts of cars, parts of shoes, parts of furniture). Other regions of former Yugoslavia bought these intermediate products and used them to make final consumer products. Because of the war, these buyers had to find new suppliers. After the war, these buyers will only come back to their pre-war suppliers if these suppliers offer the best and cheapest products available on the world market. With factories in shambles, infrastructure destroyed and workers displaced or killed, producing the best and cheapest products is not an easy task.

The war came to an end with a peace agreement that dictates a horrifyingly complex government structure. A company has to deal with several layers of government, each of which has complicated and sometimes non-sensible legislation. A simple change of business address, for example, requires procedures at the level of the municipality, canton, entity, and state. New companies face complex pre-war anti-private sector legislation and a government that provides problems rather than support in return for tax money. The only companies that benefit from the government – in the form of subsidies – are the public companies of the past. Without government support, very few of them would stay in business. In many cases, they have become uncompetitive dinosaurs, using outdated equipment and led by people chosen for their political affiliation rather than their technical expertise.

Imagine all this. It is a miracle that Bosnia and Herzegovina has some sort of functioning economy at all.

Ever since the Dayton Peace Accords were signed at the end of 1995, Bosnia and Herzegovina has been in a long, slow and painful process of economic recovery. The reform process has been slow for a number of reasons. First, there is no tested recipe for the economic revitalisation of a place that left the world economy as part of a centrally planned country and re-emerged as a war-torn independent country in a competitive free-market economy. It is simply not known what such a country should do to adapt. Second, pro-business legislation causes harm in the short run. People will lose their jobs and this is a particularly bad time to lose one's job. For obvious reasons, politicians and people will resist such legislation. Third, the focus in the immediate post-war years has been on political consolidation, not economic development. Fourth, there are very few seasoned economists available. Even the international organizations often resort to recruiting junior anthropologists to tackle issues that require senior and specialized economists. And lastly: corrupt government officials and a thriving mafia have not been helpful.

And yet, not all is bad. The currency is strong, inflation is low, the country is not heavily indebted, and much of the infrastructure has by now been reconstructed. In addition, some bad indicators do not reflect reality. At roughly 40 percent, the official unemployment rate indicates a non-functioning economy. In reality, many people registered as unemployed work in the informal sector. Similarly, the people who moved abroad have proven to be exceptionally loyal to the people they left behind. In all likelihood, they will continue to send money in the years to come. Most economists do not consider remittances a healthy economic foundation and point out that these remittances allow for the continuation of an import-based economy. True, but there is a difference between the long-term perspective and the short-term needs: the fact is that, as in other unstable (post) war parts of the world – Lebanon, the Palestinian Territories - this cash inflow does keep things afloat in times of hardship.

The next few years will be crucial. Will Bosnia and Herzegovina be able to come closer to Europe? Will the country manage to cut back its bureaucracy, privatise its public companies, and attract investments? Will logging, agriculture, steel, mining, services, textiles and building materials be the economic pillars of the future, or will new sectors arise? Will the country manage to utilise more fully its potential in agriculture (with a competitive advantage in organic farming), eco-tourism, hydro-electric power (many large dams function at only a quarter of their full potential), and wood-processing? Will the country perhaps regain its role as a producer of intermediate goods, once again supplying factories in the surrounding countries? When I look at many of the politicians, I am not very hopeful. But when I visit trade fairs and see an ever-increasing number of young companies that successfully identified market niches, I tend to think that Bosnia and Herzegovina has a bright future to look forward to.

RELIGION

In this country it is hard to find a town that doesn't have both churches and mosques. This illustrates that, indeed, Bosnia and Herzegovina is at the crossroad of eastern and western civilizations. Despite the wars, the area of Bosnia and Herzegovina has survived for over five centuries as a very multi-religious part of the world.

The medieval Bosnian church is a good starting point for understanding contemporary Bosnia and Herzegovina. Inheriting the fierce self-reliant attitude from the indigenous Illyrian clans, the newly arrived Slavic tribes adopted their own form of Christianity. While most of Europe and the Balkans were under the influence of either of the two major Christian belief systems, geographically isolated Bosnia and Herzegovina celebrated a Christian god with many elements of paganism, and without the structure and hierarchy of the organized churches. Both Catholicism and Orthodoxy vied for power in the region, but the Bosnian Church was able to maintain its unique belief system for centuries.

The arrival of the Ottomans had a more substantial religious influence on the history of Bosnia and Herzegovina than the Orthodox and Catholic submission attempts of the previous period. The first Muslims came to the region in the mid-fifteenth century, and over the next one hundred and fifty years Bosnia saw a large portion of its population convert to Islam. In the sixteenth century a fourth group entered the region. Many of the Sephardic Jews that had been expelled from Spain in 1492 resettled in Sarajevo, Mostar, Travnik and other major Bosnian cities.

In Tito's Yugoslavia, most people strayed from their religious beliefs. Religious practice was allowed but frowned upon, secularism was encouraged and the religious leaders were chosen by the communist party. For a number of reasons, the breakdown of Yugoslavia has caused a significant rise in the sense of religious belonging. First, people felt more at ease practicing their religions after the collapse of a country that was, essentially, proudly atheist. Second, a war and the suffering it causes often brings religion to the forefront. Third, this particular war was fought on ethnic lines and made many people more aware of their ethnic and thus religious identity. Fourth, and unfortunately, some of the religious revival can be attributed to nationalist agendas that use religion to inspire hatred.

Notwithstanding all the political rhetoric, the three main religious groups have influenced each other in the course of the five centuries in which they lived together. Consequently, and although many nationalists would deny it, Islam, Orthodoxy and Catholicism in Bosnia and Herzegovina are quite different from Islam, Orthodoxy and Catholicism anywhere else. Believers of each group often have more in common with their fellow-Bosnians than with their fellow-believers in other countries.

CULTURE

Some museums are good, but the exhibits of even the best ones do not match the power of the cultural manifestations that you will find every-where in everyday life. Many of these cultural manifestations have this little twist that makes them unique to Bosnia and Herzegovina. Mosques around the world shy away from depicting living things, but the multi-colored mosque in Travnik has elaborate flower scenes painted on the outside. The tombstones that line the countryside show roughly carved people with very large hands – something I have not seen anywhere else in the world. Many houses have no paintings at all, but many others have paintings covering their walls three rows high. Order a plate of meat or fish for a group of people and you will get an artfully composed and humorous mountain of niceties.

In Bosnia and Herzegovina, concepts are pursued until the very end. You see it in literature, where themes are considered from every possible side before the story goes on. You see it in the eye for detail when people dress up. You see it in the composition and variety of a mixed grill. You see it in the copper market in Ferhadija, where anything made of metal – trays, coffee sets, and even bullets and mortars - can be turned into a piece of art.

On the other hand, simplicity is treasured. A Turkish table, an Egyp-tian tray or a Palestinian dress are all about complexity and detail. Not an inch of material is left uncarved, uncut, unembroidered. Bosnia and Herzegovina shares the same Ottoman heritage, but its tables, trays and attires look decidedly different. They focus on beauty, not complexity. No-Man's Land, the Oscar-winning movie about the war, illustrates that this ability to transmit no-frill messages is still very much alive. The entire war is reduced to three men in a trench.

Art

There are very few cave paintings in Europe older than 14,000 years. The carvings in the Badanj Caves in southern Herzegovina are among them. Closely followed by pottery and artfully sculpted figures (on display at the National Museum in Sarajevo), they are the oldest art yet discovered in Bosnia and Herzegovina.

More refined art forms were taken from the Greeks and the Romans. In the Hellenistic and Roman eras, the Daorsi tribe - ahead of the other tribes - sometimes sided with and was influenced by both. The Daorsi left Hellenistic town remnants and moulds from jewelers' workshops. They introduced the symbols of early Christianity to the region, and left behind beautiful basilicas and mosaics.

These Paleolithic, Neolithic, Hellenistic and Roman remains are inter-esting, but do not yet show Bosnia and Herzegovina's unique face. That face appears in the medieval times. A new script appears – bosančica – and there are the symbols and art forms of the Bosnian church. Perhaps the most inspiring of these are the engraved tombstones, stećci in Bosnian, that still dot the countryside. These stećci, with pagan and Christian sym-bols of earth, moon, family, animals, dance and crosses, form a permanent reminder of the early Slavs' creativity.

Four centuries of Ottoman rule had a profound impact on the region. The many Ottoman bridges, mosques, markets, houses, libraries, dervish convents, streets and trading route resting places still give the country a decidedly oriental feel. Many of these Ottoman treasures are outside or can be visited. In the same period, the Christians painted the frescoes, icons and paintings that can be seen in the country's many monasteries. The orthodox monasteries of Paprača, Lomnica, Dobričevo, Žitomislići and Trijebanj and the Catholic monasteries of Kraljeva Sutjeska, Fojnica, Kreševo, Olovo, Gorica and Toliša are all well worth a visit.

Contemporary art has been influenced by all that preceded it. The Ottoman heritage lives forth in the work of the copper, gold, silver and leather crafts, and in the paintings of Safet Zec (famous for his delicate paintings of the oriental feel of a European Bosnia) and Mersad Berber (who portrays Muslim life in works such as Chronicle About Sarajevo). Other painters such as Gabriel Jurkić and Karlo Mijić and the abstract work of Affan Ramić depict the natural wonders of the Bosnian landscape, demonstrating the intimate ties between man and nature.

The war shines through in much of the most recent work of artists around the country. Artists display expressions of resistance, hope and peace. Sculpture, paintings, graffiti and graphic design all portray the new generation's struggle to heal the wounds of the past and rid the collective consciousness of the lunacy of the war.

Film

Bosnia and Herzegovina has produced some of the finest films to come out of the former Yugoslavia. Even Emir Kusturica, the great filmmaker from Serbia, was born and raised here. The modern film scene has taken off with the production of Danis Tanović's No-Man's Land (Ničija zemlja), this country's first-ever Oscar winning movie. In this brilliant tragic comedy, a few opposing soldiers, stuck in an abandoned trench between frontlines, represent the entire war. All is lost. In the end, the last man is left to die, unseen by the media, while an incompetent international representative walks away claiming a successful operation. In the back you hear a Bosnian bedtime song. Go to sleep. All is well.

Other striking movies, mostly about the war, include Perfect Circle (Savršeni krug) by Ademir Kenović, Fuse (Gori vatra) by Pjer Žalica, Re-Make by Dino Mustafić, and Summer in the Golden Valley (Ljeto u zlatnoj dolini), the 2004 winner of the Rotterdam Film Festival Tiger award. One of the latest Bosnian film productions is "Kod amidže Idriza", written by Namik Kabil and directed by Pjer Žalica. The film is a magnificent depiction of the peculiar and pronounced details of a Muslim family from Sarajevo. The attention to detail – particularly Bosnian cuisine and the inability of males to express their emotions - makes it a slow film, but one you don't want to end. If true insight into the heart of a typical Sarajevo family interests you, go see this film.

Literature

Ever since Ottoman times, Bosnia and Herzegovina has been a country of books. Muslim scholars, Serbian priests and Franciscan monks all contributed to Bosnia and Herzegovina's literary tradition.

Throughout the centuries, what shone through most writings was a strong sense of patriotism, the spirit of self-reliance, and the moral issues related to the political and social abuses suffered by all three peoples.

The most important pre-20th century authors

Mustafa Ejubović	Islamic scholarly thought.
Ahmed Sudi	Islamic scholarly thought.
Fevzi Mostarac	Wrote the famous Bulbulistan in 18th-century Persian.
Mula Mustafa Bašeskija	Wrote a diary of life in Sarajevo in the last half of the 1700s. He wrote it in a unique Turkish dialect that was only spoken in Sarajevo.
Hasan Kaimija	A poet who gained popularity as a defender of common folk.
Fra Matija Divković	Wrote the first published book in bosančica in Bosnia and Herzegovina in 1611 (printed in Venice).
Brother Filip Lastrić	The best-known historian of the Bosna Srebrena province. He wrote books that preserved the heritage of the old Bosnian State.
Nicifor Dučić	An orthodox monk who published nine volumes of historical works.
Joanikije Pamučina	Portrayed folklore and history in the Glorious Martyrdom of the Virgin Hristina Rajković.
Gavro Vučković Krajišnik	Wrote Slavery in Freedom or Mirror of Justice in Bosnia and The Bloody Book of Brother Ante Knežević. Both books were banned by the Ottoman government.
Vaso Pelagić	This was the greatest of the 19th-century Bosnian Serb writers. He stood out not only for his literary skill but also as one of the sharpest thinkers and political figures of his time.
Ivan Franjo Jukić	This Franciscan from Banja Luka personified the freedom struggle and wrote great works in many genres reflecting the emancipation movement that dominated 19th-century life in Bosnia and Herzegovina.

In the early twentieth century, many newspapers were established and Bosnian writers were fully exposed to European thought for the first time. After more than four centuries of Ottoman and Austrian rule, a struggle for national identity dominated the literature of this period. It was this struggle that had polarizing effects on the future of Bosnia. On the one hand it paved the way for the union of the southern Slavs. On the other hand it created ethnic rifts amongst the Slavs through the intensity of the nationalist voices which emerged. Ivo Andrić began his writing career in this period.

Alongside the nationalist fervor was the liberal movement of writers in The Comrades Book. This left-wing movement, with a passion for the social issues of the time, produced famous writers such as Novak Šimić, Hasan Kikić and Mak Dizdar. They were catalysts for the cultural revolution of the second half of the 20th century.

The greatest writers in Bosnia's history emerged post World War II in socialist Yugoslavia. Ivo Andrić continued his literary domination in the Bridge over the Drina, Travnik Chronicles and The Damned Yard. In 1961 he was awarded the Nobel Prize for Literature. Soon after, Mak Dizdar and Meša Selimović published two of Bosnia's most famous pieces: Stone Sleeper and Death and the Derviš. In the late sixties yet more masterpieces were published: Nedžad Ibrišimović's Ugursuz, Vitomir Lukić's Album, Skender Kulenović's first book of sonnets, and Branko Ćopić's book of stories The Blue Mallow Garden.

In post-war Bosnia the leading literary thinkers are Aleksandar Hemon, Nenad Veličković, Faruk Šehić, Dario Džamonja, Dževad Karahasan and Marko Vešović. Philosopher and writer Ivan Lovrenović offers one of the most insightful and objective viewpoints in Bosnian intellectual circles. For moving war accounts, read Miljenko Jergović's Sarajevo Marlboro and Zlata Maglajlić's Zlata's Diary. There are many others. They are now scattered across the globe, but their themes and inspiration tend to remain close to home.

The books of many of the writers mentioned here have been translated into English. Some of these books are available at the few bookshops in the country that have a sizeable English language selection.

Music

There are countries where a group of people who spend the evening together enjoy themselves talking or dancing. In Bosnia and Herzegovina, people tend to sing. For an outsider, it is a joy to watch. After an hour or so, somebody starts a 'sevdalinka', and the tone of the evening has been set: there is no more talking from that moment onwards. Instead, songs come and go, with or without instruments, for hours and hours. In just one voice, everybody sings the same nostalgic folk songs about life before the war. And everybody seems to know them all.

Most of this folk music traces its origins to Ottoman times and combines oriental elements with the popular heritage of Bosnia and Herzegovina. Most of these songs are songs of love and tragedy. They helped to get through turbulent times.

The sounds of the highlanders are equally fascinating. The music of the Dinaric shepherds has echoed through the mountain valleys for centuries. This type of mountain yodel is called ojkanje and is a mixed melody of male and female 'oi' sounds. Highlanders have always celebrated in open fields with the 'gluho kolo' or deaf dance. The villages' young bachelors and girls gather for a large circle dance accompanied by song. This ceremony continues through the night. It is often the setting for courting.

Then there is the ganga, a deep, non-instrumental, chant-like music most often sung by Croat men in Herzegovina. There is the Serbian gusle, a type of banjo, that accompanies century-old stories. There are the šargija instruments of the northwest of the country, and there is the Persian saz that most commonly accompanies traditional music in the cities. It's all unique to this region, and it's all equally tantalizing.

There is contemporary music as well. Famous groups from the old Yugoslavia are still held in high regard and their songs still crowd the airwaves. Groups like Bijelo dugme, Zabranjeno pušenje, Indexi and Crvena jabuka represent the climax of Yugoslav 1980s rock. Yesterday's and today's most famous pop stars are probably Dino Merlin and Kemal Monteno. With very different musical styles, they both enjoy huge popularity with young and old.

Sarajevo is the centre of Bosnia and Herzegovina's modern music scene but there are great bands from Mostar, Tuzla and Banja Luka as well. Mostar Sevdah Reunion is a magnificent band with a smooth mix of jazz, blues and a touch of tradition. Jazz bands and clubs have become increasingly popular and every November Sarajevo hosts a great International Jazz Festival. Digital music has hit the scene with Adi Lukovac i Ornamenti and others. But the tradition of rock and alternative music never died, and groups like Knock-Out, Kiks, Tifa, Sikter, and Protest still attract big crowds and play at venues throughout the country. Skroz and Dubioza kolektiv are the most popular new emerging bands.

Classical music, *by Keziah Conrad*

Sarajevans often pride themselves on sophisticated cultural tastes, including an appreciation for high-quality classical music. This music represents civilization, a link with the wider Western world— but more than that, it signifies beauty, passion, life, hope in the face of the darkest night. Many outsiders are familiar with the story of Vedran Smailović, a cellist in the Sarajevo Philharmonic Orchestra, who defiantly played on the streets and in ruined buildings while bombs and bullets rained down. Musicians have been a crucial part of the restoration of Sarajevo, giving voice to suffering, offering healing through beauty, taking part in projects that cross borders and lead toward reconciliation.

Three institutions are prominent in Sarajevo's classical music scene: the National Theater (with its Philharmonic Orchestra, Opera and Ballet), the Music Academy of Sarajevo University, and "JU Sarajevo Art", which coordinates performances of artists from Bosnia and Herzegovina and beyond. Sarajevo's National Theater opened in 1921, and since that time has been the scene of thousands of theatrical and musical performances. In 2004, musical events produced by the National Theater have included Mozart's *Requiem*, Orff's *Carmina Burana*, Beethoven's 5th Symphony, Verdi's *Nabucco*, Horozić's *Hasanaginica*, and a world premiere of Čavlović's opera *The Women of Srebrenica*. Sarajevo

Art organizes the annual summer festival Baščaršian Nights and an ongoing program of performances by local and international artists.

A range of amateur choirs and cultural societies perform regularly around the country. Several of these, such as Pontanima Interreligious Choir and the women's ensembles Gaudeamus and Allegra, have earned international recognition for their musicianship. Other groups include the choirs of the Cathedral, the Orthodox Church, and the Islamic *medresa* (school of theology).

Classical music in Bosnia and Herzegovina faces severe underfunding and a demoralizing lack of resources that has forced many prominent musicians to leave—but many others have stayed and are still working with passion and talent. Visiting artists and audience members often observe that musicians from this country have an electric energy and striking depth of feeling that is not easy to find elsewhere. Perhaps this is the product of artistry honed by suffering; a living vibrancy that arises out of intimate experience with death.

HISTORY

The history of the region of the former Yugoslavia has, for many, been a bewildering subject. Perhaps the most important thing to keep in mind while trying to fit the pieces of the Bosnian puzzle into a coherent context, is that the nationalist sentiments that were born at the end of the nineteenth century and are alive today, do not reflect the life and sentiments of the tiny, isolated communities of this country from the seventh to thirteenth centuries. The 'mental baggage' that is carried today by Serbs, Croats or Muslims can simply not be applied to a population which previously held no affiliation to a national or ethnic identity. The Orthodox from eastern Herzegovina did not wave a Serbian flag, the Catholics from Bosna srebrena did not have dreams of coming under Zagreb's rule, and the converted Muslim community had no aspirations to create a European Mecca in the heart of Bosnia. It is largely unknown whether the original Slav settlers, well into the Middle Ages, even referred to themselves at all as Serbs or Croats. All too often history is the story of kings and queens, conquerors and defenders, and provides little if any understanding of the life of the ordinary people. The early Slav tribes never engaged in bitter debates or wars over their Serbian or Croatian belonging; they lived in peace with each other, spoke the same language and worshipped the same god. Outside influences often divided communities but the impetus for such divisions never came from within.

In the historical context of Bosnia and Herzegovina much is still argued over, both domestically and internationally. What no one can debate, however, is today's rightful claim of all the peoples of Bosnia and Herzegovina to call this their home. Serbs, Croats and Bosniacs (the term used for Bosnian Muslims, identifying nationality and not religion) can confidently say that their homeland is Bosnia and Herzegovina and that they have been here for many, many generations. Claiming rightful ownership of one group over another from a historical perspective, with all its complexities, is simply an impossibility.

Ancient History

The territory of Bosnia and Herzegovina is profusely scattered with remnants of human life that spans the period from the Paleolithic age to the emergence of the Illyrian clan alliances.

Research into the Stone Age indicates that the northern parts of Bosnia and Herzegovina near the Bosna, Ukrina and Usora rivers were the most developed at that time. The leap from Neanderthal man in the middle Paleolithic, to the homo sapiens of the Late Paleolithic is signified by the first cave drawing of that period, found in Badanj Cave near Stolac in Herzegovina. This rare sample is dated at 12,000BC and there have been similar finds in only three other locations: Spain, France and Italy. The end of the Paleolithic Age saw tremendous climatic change, changes so drastic that much of human life disappeared from this area until about 4,000BC.

After this long, dark Mesolithic period a rich Neolithic culture developed in the third millennium BC. Conditions were ideal for the formation of settlements that developed a new kind of social organization and enjoyed over a millennium of continuity. Many of the fine pottery and arts and crafts of this age are on display in the National Museum in Sarajevo. This highly skilled culture signified a golden age where spiritual life was matched by creative talent. The ancient settlement of Butmir, presently a suburb south of Sarajevo at the base of Igman Mountain, can alone testify to the craftsmanship achieved in that territory by Neolithic man. This unique Neolithic culture disappeared from Bosnia and Herzegovina without a trace somewhere between the third and second millennia BC.

A great metamorphosis swept across the Balkans in a movement that began with the arrival of nomadic tribes from the Black Sea steppes. With their arrival to the Balkans came a new Copper Age. This Aeneolithic period saw a parallel development of stone and metal. The use of metal became increasingly valuable for weapon making, as well-armed tribes from west Pannonia expanded south and southeast towards the end of the second millennium. Wars became more frequent, and Bosnia became very popular for the sanctuary its deep valleys, thick forests and rugged mountains provided.

Illyrians

The first few centuries of the first millennium BC in Bosnia and Herzegovina, as throughout the entire western Balkan Peninsula, saw the gradual creation of a broad ethnic and cultural foundation. From the tribes belonging to the Iron Age culture emerged an ethnic group that history has collectively named the Illyrians.

The Illyrian tribes settled across a large swathe of the western Balkans from the Adriatic Coast in the west to the river Morava in the east, and from present day Albania in the south to the Istrian Peninsula in what today is northwest Croatia. These loosely bound tribes began to form new territorial and economic ties in the middle of the first millennium BC. This process appears to have been the most profound amongst the southern Illyrian tribes, including those tribes of present day Bosnia and Herzegovina.

The Celtic migration inland and the Greek colonies established on the Adriatic Coast in the 4th Century BC, marked a new and painful chapter in Illyrian history. These events brought about significant cultural and spiritual change. It also increased the desire of the Roman Empire to expand and conquer these areas.

The Romans attacked in 229BC, first capturing the islands and crushing the Illyrian navy. In 168BC the famous Illyrian king Gentius was defeated and this gave the Romans a stronghold on Illyrian soil. The inland tribes of Illyria, however, put up a ferocious fight and it took a century and a half of the Romans' best commanders and military forces to defeat the defiant clans. Finally, from 35-33BC, under the direct command of Emperor Octavian, the Roman army launched a major attack that, after the Emperor himself was seriously wounded from a guerilla attack, forced the surrender of the Dalmati clan. The coastal clans were by and large conquered by the overwhelming size of the Roman army.

In the last 'battle royal' for the inland territories held by the Illyrian tribes in what is the heart of present day Bosnia, the clan alliances staged what is known as the *Batonian Uprising*. Two namesakes of large Illyrian tribes united to fend off the invaders. Panicked by the rumors that there were '800,000 insurgents, including 200,000 elite warriors and 9,000 horsemen', Emperor Augustus sent two of his top commanders, Tiberius and Germanicus, to subdue and conquer the fierce and stubborn Illyrians. The fighting went on for years, with both sides exchanging defeats and victories. The last Illyrian stronghold to fall was the citadel at Vranduk near the central Bosnian city of Zenica. According to Roman records, when the Illyrian leader Batan surrendered, the Illyrian women, holding their children, threw themselves into the fire to avoid being captured and enslaved. The Romans incorporated the two Illyrian provinces of Pannonia and Dalmatia into their empire. Some extremely isolated remnants of Illyrian tribes probably survived and eventually assimilated with the Slavs when they arrived in the 7th century.

There are still a few archeological sites that mark the Illyrian civilization in Bosnia and Herzegovina. Many of the Illyrian fortifications were expanded upon by the Romans and later by the Bosnian aristocracy and the Ottomans. New research, however, has uncovered a fascinating aspect of Illyria. At Vranduk in central Bosnia, Blagaj near the Buna River in Herzegovina and on the Cyclopean walls at Osanići near Stolac, finds have indicated that the culture of antiquity came long before the Romans, most likely in Hellenistic form. Osanići was home to the Daorsi tribe and recent archeological findings point to a third century BC link to a northerly extension of the great Hellenistic civilization.

Much of Illyrian culture will forever remain a mystery but one cannot deny the spiritual and cultural impact it has had, even almost two millennia after their disappearance.

Ancient Illyricum

With the fall of the Illyrian clan alliances to the Romans, the territory of present day Bosnia and Herzegovina became part of the vast Roman Empire.

The early period of Roman occupation was peaceful and stable. There were, of course, some tribes who rejected Roman rule but for the most part the efficient Romans quickly set aim at taming Illyricum to cater to the Empire's needs. A Roman administration was established and the task of building roads, mining for iron, gold, lead and rock and mobilizing a large labor force and military were the first priorities. The Illyrians were actively recruited into the Roman army.

The most populated areas continued to be the Empire's regional centers. By the third century AC Illyricum had flourished into a proper Roman province. Its people had equal standing within the Empire and could even aspire to political office. Although Christianity was introduced and largely accepted, elements of Illyrium pagan beliefs were maintained and passed on.

With the disintegration of the western Empire in the fifth century much of the Illyrian lands fell into the hands of the Ostrogoths. The Illyrians again enjoyed a period of relative peace and stability but by the mid-6th century the eastern Empire was able to regain most of the Illyrian lands. As the Roman Empire declined new attacks occurred on the northern frontiers, this time from the Avars and Slavs.

After several centuries of drastic social change in Europe a mélange of cultures made their mark on present day Bosnia and Herzegovina. Basilicas from the late Roman period can be found as their use was continued by the new settlements of Slavs. Remains can be found in Čapljina, Blagaj and Ljubuški in Herzegovina; Breza, Zenica, Travnik and Kiseljak in central Bosnia; and Banja Luka and Mrkonjić Grad in the northwest of the country.

The Slavs

With the fall of the western Empire the new era in Bosnia and Herzegovina was largely dominated by the Slavs. From the sixth century onwards sizeable Slav migration flows came from the east. The Avars gradually retreated to Pannonia but the Slavs remained in their new homeland. It is this ethnic group that most of present day Bosnia and Herzegovina's ethnic make-up is based upon.

Historical evidence of the first centuries of Slav settlements in the area of Bosnia and Herzegovina is practically non-existent. The first recorded evidence of Bosnia and Herzegovina under the Slavs dates from the tenth century. Several centuries later a Byzantine writer stated that 'Bosnia is not a vassal state but is independent, the people lead their own life and rule themselves.'

Graveyards have become the most important source of information about the culture of this time. Archeological digs in older necropolises have unearthed locally made jewellery and weapons from the Slav period. A unique aspect of this time was the development of skilled work with stone. This art would later surface in what is seen today as a national trademark of Bosnia and Herzegovina – the *stećak* (plural *stećci*). These medieval tombstones were elaborately carved with drawings depicting Christian and pagan beliefs. *Stećci* date from the eleventh to the thirteenth centuries and can be found today at dozens of locations all over Bosnia and Herzegovina. These tombstones are unique to this part of the world.

Medieval Bosnia

The early Middle Ages placed the southern Slavs in a very precarious position – wedged between the two great cultural bodies of eastern and western Christianity. Both Byzantium and Rome set out to influence the political and religious structure of this crossroads region. The geographical position of the southern Slavs became an important factor in the eleventh century split between the Orthodox and Catholic churches. Both churches asserted their influences and left a permanent mark on the region's cultural history.

The spiritual culture that developed in medieval Bosnia was very similar to that of its Illyrian predecessors. There was a large degree of cultural resistance and fierce independence that resulted in a creative mold of Christianity. In a relatively inaccessible and isolated area emerged what was to be a unique form of Christianity in medieval Europe – the Bosnian church. Whilst still influenced by the great divide and spread of Orthodoxy and Catholicism the Bosnian church, along with its own alphabet – *bosančica* (similar to both Glagolithic and Cyrillic) - flourished in the medieval Bosnian state. In an era that saw Europe dominated by religious exclusiveness, Bosnia was able to maintain a high level of secularism in all spheres of life.

Cultural development in medieval Bosnia

Written records don't show how the ordinary persons lived, what lifestyle they enjoyed, and what cultural heritage developed in medieval Bosnia. What we do know is that many unique forms of language, art, literature, and worship evolved in Bosnia during the Middle Ages.

The key to Bosnia's wealth was its copper, silver, lead, gold and other natural resources. Copper and silver were mined at Kreševo and Fojnica in central Bosnia; lead was mined in Olovo to the northeast of Sarajevo; and gold, silver and lead in were mined in Zvornik on the River Drina. The most significant and productive area in all of Bosnia and Herzegovina was the silver mine at Srebrenica. A large working class developed around this industry, some of which can still be found today.

During the Middle Ages Bosnia became a very important trading route. Merchants from both east and west moved and traded their goods through or in Bosnian territory. Trading towns and routes sprung up or rejuvenated in Visoko, Jajce, Travnik, Goražde and Livno. Many locals became involved in trade, particularly with Ragusa (Dubrovnik). Bosnia and Dubrovnik today still share close cultural ties.

A unique alphabet evolved in medieval Bosnia. Cyrillic and Glagolithic had been introduced in the tenth century and a special form of Cyrillic developed during the middle-ages. Glagolithic and Cyrillic were used simultaneously for some time, both copying texts and manuscripts from each other. The use of these two alphabets slowly merged into one - Bosnian Cyrillic or *bosančica.* It became the most commonly used alphabet in later medieval times.

Whereas most literature in medieval Europe came from clergy and monasteries, Bosnian writings were remarkably secular. The most famous of these is the Kulin Charter of 1189, written to the people of Dubrovnik. This was the first official act written in the national language of the Slavic south. Many documents show that it was not only the nobility but merchants and craftsmen who reached a relatively high level of literacy. There are, however, also many religious documents from this time. Examples include the Cyrillic *Miroslav Missal*, produced by the Duke of Hum in the 12th century, the *Divoš Tihoradić Gospel* from the 14th century and the *Čajniče Gospel* which is the only medieval codex still in existence in Bosnia today. These manuscripts used a wealth of human and animal miniatures all drawn in a unique south Slav style. The Franciscan monastery in Kraljeva

Sutjeska possesses some of the earliest written works and the first bible, complete with the *bosančica* alphabet. They can be viewed in the museum and library in this small town in central Bosnia.

Art took many forms in medieval Bosnia. Silver, gold, bronze and copper were used, particularly in the 14th and 15th centuries, for jewellery making, costumes, coins, bowls, and other artifacts. Many of the designs resemble Romanesque-Gothic styles, some with an eastern mystical flavor. The most important art of medieval Bosnia, though, was the stonework of the *stećci* (gravestones). These unique gravestones from Bosnia and Hum are not found anywhere else in Europe.

In different styles, these *stećci* portray crosses, swords, symbols of purity, and anthropomorphic symbols (dance, traditional attire, sacred symbols, deer, horses). The Bosnian Cyrillic script showed its most artistic face on these *stećci*. But the most remarkable trait of the *stećci* is their poetic and philosophical power. They stand apart from any known conventional European burial rites. They are found mostly in Bosnia and Herzegovina but there are also *stećci* in Dalmatia, the Croatian hinterland, western Serbia and Montenegro – all within the boundaries of the former Bosnian State. This art form continued into Ottoman times and well into the 16th century, with some of the later *stećci* including Islamic symbols.

Bosnia and Herzegovina is a living gallery of the stone art of the middle-ages. Over 60,000 *stećci* tombstones are dotted throughout the country with the largest necropolis at Radimlja near the Herzegovinian town of Stolac. Mak Dizdar, the most famous of Bosnian poets, wrote frequently of the *stećci* and their meaning in *Kameni spavač*, the *Stone Sleeper*. Whether or not his interpretations of the *stećci* are right, they remain a national symbol of Bosnia and Herzegovina.

It should be well noted that most of medieval European history does not see it fit to mention much of the contributions of women during this time. The mainly male dominant and patriarchal depiction of this era is to say the least unfair – as women have always made significant contributions in art, agriculture, family life, and even male dominated politics. The authors do not wish to exclude women by any means but have simply been unable to unearth their major contributions of this time. What we do know is that women in the region of Bosnia and Herzegovina at this time were not persecuted as witches as were their counterparts in much of western Europe.

Ottoman rule

In the summer of 1463 the Ottoman army, after years of penetration into Bosnian territory, captured the Bosnian banate and the region around Sarajevo. These lands would be in more or less firm Ottoman control for the next four centuries. Many of the gains in the northern half of Bosnia, however, were reversed by King Mathias of Hungary. He established a northern banate under Hungarian rule and named the Bosnian 'ban' King of Bosnia. The kingdom slowly dwindled as Ottoman incursions wore down the resistance, and by the 1520s the kingdom's capital, Jajce, came under constant siege until it fell in 1528.

Herzegovina also succeeded in repelling the Ottomans for some time after 1463. Herceg Stjepan Vukčić held most of Herzegovina for the next two years, until another swarming invasion sent him into exile in Novi (later named Herceg-Novi in his honor), Montenegro. His son Vlatko attempted to enlist the help of the Hungarians and Venetians but internal strife with local noblemen and neighboring Ragusa enabled the Ottomans to take a strong hold by the 1470s, and in 1482 the last fortress in Herzegovina was overrun.

The Ottomans conquered territories, particularly in the north towards Europe, not to convert the inhabitants, but for the land, for acquiring new conscripts for further Ottoman gains, and for the taxes the Empire could impose to wage these wars. Besides conquering Bosnia and Herzegovina, Mehmed II destroyed the Venetian army in Greece, began making incursions into Moldavia and Hungary, and was on the verge of launching a full scale invasion of Italy when he died in 1481. His successor, Bayezit II, continued consolidating Ottoman gains. Suleyman the Magnificent's rule from 1520-1566 managed to reduce Hungary to the status of a vassal territory and the Ottomans came inches away from capturing Vienna. The 1533 peace treaty with Austria established a long and static confrontation line between the Hapsburg and Ottoman Empires. Each side spent years building up their respective frontier zones, thus assuring that Bosnia's borders did not see heavy military activity until the Sultan waged war on the Hapsburgs in 1566. Military campaigns continued from 1593 to 1606. The Ottoman presence in Bosnia was a military enterprise from where major offensives against the Hapsburgs were launched.

In the course of 150 years, more and more of Bosnia's inhabitants converted to Islam. The Islamicization of the Bosnian population is possibly the most distinctive and maybe the most important event in its history. There was, and still is, a lot of controversy surrounding this issue, with most arguments being based on myth and folklore. Although one will still find today bitter 'memories' of 'forced' conversion, the process as a whole did not largely come by force or through war.

While the evidence available does not prove that there was a policy of forced conversions, this is not to say that there was no persecution and oppression of Christians. The Orthodox Church, falling under the jurisdiction of the Ottoman Empire, was an accepted institution. The Catholic Church, the church of the enemy Austrians, was treated with a heavier hand. In the geographical territory of Bosnia at the time of the Ottoman conquest, there were few Orthodox communities. They grew in size during the Ottoman occupation. Conversely, there were an estimated 35 Franciscan monasteries in Bosnia and Herzegovina before the invasion, but by the mid-1600s only ten remained.

The religious practices of both the Bosnian Christians and Muslims point to a mystical convergence of the two faiths. Even today, Christians and Muslims share the same superstitions in the power of amulets, with many Muslims having them blessed by Franciscan monks. Many holy days and festivals were celebrated by both religious communities. 'Muslim' ceremonies were often conducted in Christian churches and masses were held in front of the Virgin Mary to cure or ward off illness. There are records of Christians calling for Muslim dervishes to read verses from the Qu'ran to cure or bless them. It is quite clear that a synthesis of diverging beliefs occurred in Bosnia and Herzegovina, where 'all sects meet on a common basis of secular superstition.'

Most of Bosnia and Herzegovina's present day cities and towns were created during the Ottoman period. A focus on building towns and constructing roads and bridges to connect these towns brought the whole country, for the first time, into an urbanized sphere. Never before had any central administration effectively embarked on a vision of building a country. Islamic art and culture added a remarkable aspect to life in Bosnia and Herzegovina. Unlike the often brutal feudal systems seen elsewhere in Europe at that time, the Ottoman Empire allowed the Orthodox Church and the new Jewish community to enjoy growth and prosperity.

A small community of Sephardic Jews who had been expelled from Spain in 1492 settled in Sarajevo, Travnik and Mostar, and was tolerated by the Ottomans. Jewish merchants quickly established themselves in the textile and silk trades. This tradition would stand until the destruction of the Jewish community in the Second World War. They were skilled metal workers and it is believed that the Anatolian Jews greatly advanced Ottoman weaponry. For this priceless gift it is said that the Jews were given their own mahala in Sarajevo near the central market. Several synagogues and a hram were built. From an early stage after their arrival, the Jews of Bosnia and Herzegovina played an important role in the cultural and religious life of the cities where they settled.

The decline of the Ottoman Empire

A major Ottoman defeat at the hands of the Austrians in 1683 signaled a drastic decline in the Empire. In 1697 Eugene of Savoy advanced on Bosnia and reached Sarajevo. Sarajevo was put to the torch and most of the town went up in flames. When he retreated many Catholics left with his army for fear of reprisals. This decimated the Catholic population and only three Franciscan monasteries remained open. The frontier lands in the Krajina were in constant conflict, and unrest in eastern Herzegovina along the Montenegrin border became commonplace

At the turn of the nineteenth century Napoleon and France defeated Austria and took over Venetia, Istria and Dalmatia. Austria again declared war on France in 1809 and by 1813 Austria ruled those areas again. The biggest threat, however, was no longer the Austrians but the powerful rebellions to the east in Serbia. Large-scale revolts took place in which Slav Muslims were massacred. The Ottomans granted Serbia a greater amount of autonomy in 1815. By the end of the Napoleonic wars it became clear to Istanbul that the Empire was so weak that it would collapse without aggressive reform. Now fighting battles on all fronts it was too difficult for the Ottomans to reestablish control of Bosnia. Bosnia's local governors and military leaders looked for more autonomy and began making demands to the Ottoman authorities. Many local militias offered the Ottomans military assistance but with strict demands on self-rule and insisting that taxes levied by the Empire be waived. Christians and Muslims alike were seeking sweeping reforms within the Empire. A final blow was struck in a massive revolt that lasted three years from 1875 to 1878. This revolt effectively ended Ottoman rule in Bosnia and Herzegovina. Russia had declared war on the Ottoman Empire in 1877, and the earlier plans of the Austrians and Russians would soon become reality. By October 20, 1878 the total occupation of Bosnia and Herzegovina was complete. A new era under Austro-Hungarian rule began.

Austro-Hungarian rule

The Congress of Berlin redrew the map of the Balkans and approved the Austro-Hungarian occupation of Bosnia and Herzegovina in 1878, and the

Austro-Hungarians wasted no time in establishing their rule.

By holding the territory of Bosnia and Herzegovina, Austro-Hungary acquired great economic and market potential. More importantly, it enabled the empire to effectively establish an opposition to Russian influence in the Balkans. They were able to keep a close watch on Serbia and could begin 'experimenting' on an even greater ambition – expansion to the east. These factors shaped Austro-Hungarian policy in Bosnia and Herzegovina. Austro-Hungarian rule allowed the feudal system, however backwards and outdated, to continue and govern everyday life. Meanwhile, progressive and modern measures in certain spheres of life were rapidly embarked upon.

The most visible changes under Austro-Hungarian occupation were the introduction of European styles of architecture, cuisine, behavior, and dress, and the population reshuffle. Lacking confidence in the native inhabitants, foreign officials, mainly Slav, assumed the administrative duties of governing the state. Large numbers of peasants from the Empire's other territories were brought into Bosnia and Herzegovina's already overwhelmingly peasant population. Muslims from Bosnia and Herzegovina emigrated south and east on a massive scale as the Empire implemented a policy of rebalancing the country's religious make-up.

Within the framework of a new colonial policy, widespread and rapid social change and national diversification occurred. These changes fueled national and political antagonisms so powerful that even the mighty Austro-Hungarian Empire could not keep them at bay. It was not so much an organized agenda of political affiliation but rather a spontaneous expression, largely by youth, of a revolutionary spirit. Nationalist agendas did arise in the beginning of the 20th century but the general resistance was more at a class level than at a national one. Acts of terrorism began when Bosnia and Herzegovina was officially annexed in 1908. In 1910, there was a failed assassination attempt on Emperor Franz Joseph. In the same year the governor of Bosnia and Herzegovina, general Marijan Varešanin, was shot, and in June 1914 a young Serbian nationalist by the name of Gavrilo Princip shot dead Prince Ferdinand and his pregnant wife on a bridge in Sarajevo. This event not only sparked the end of Austro-Hungarian rule in Bosnia and Herzegovina, but also led to the large political fallouts between the great powers that preceded the first battles of World War I.

Austro-Hungary's declaration of war on Serbia on July 28, 1914 carved deep wounds and strengthened aged alliances amongst the world powers. Bosnians and Herzegovinians were sent to fight against the regime that repressed them.

The Kingdom of Serbs, Croats, and Slovenes and the First Yugoslavia

Towards the end of WWI the Austro-Hungarians attempted to 'rearrange' the status of Bosnia and Herzegovina. The governor of Bosnia and Herzegovina, Baron Sarkotić, suggested to the Emperor that the country join with Croatia or be granted special autonomy under the Hungarian crown. As the war efforts continued to falter towards the end of 1918, the idea of Bosnia and Herzegovina remaining under Austro-Hungarian rule was completely abandoned and talks of the creation of a Yugoslav state began. The leader of the Bosnian Muslims, Mehmed Spaho, had the task of uniting the divided loyalties of the Muslim populations. Although some disparities still existed amongst the Muslims he declared the Muslims of Bosnia and Herzegovina were in favor of a Yugoslav state. National Councils were formed, first in Zagreb and then in Bosnia and Herzegovina, renouncing the rule of the Hapsburgs in countries formerly under Austro-Hungarian authority. Days later, Croatia, Bosnia and Herzegovina and Slovenia joined with the Kingdom of Serbia to form the Kingdom of Serbs, Croats, and Slovenes. Within this new kingdom, Croatia, as well as the Bosnian Muslims and Bosnian Croats, sought some sort of regional self-governance. The Kingdom of Serbia, supported by the Bosnian Serbs, did not feel for that and established a centralist style rule from Belgrade.

Resistance against the Serb domination mounted, and in 1932 the leader of the Croatian party, Vlatko Maček, issued a 'Resolution' calling for a return to democracy and the end of Serbian hegemony. The Slovenian and Bosnian leaders followed suit with similar statements and all three were subsequently arrested. Their arrests did not go down well, and in 1934 King Aleksandar was assassinated. A year later his successor, Prince Paul, ordered new elections. The resulting loose new alliance lasted a shaky four years and ended when a Serbian minister asserted to parliament in a speech that the 'Serb policies will always be the policies of this house and this government.' Later that evening five key ministers resigned and the government imploded.

Hitler had by now begun advancing on Czechoslovakia, and his devout admirer Ante Pavelić in Italy was pushing for the break-up of Yugoslavia. It was apparent that there was a desperate need for the Serbs to bring the Croats back on board and to find a solution the Croats would accept. Cvetković and Maček met and began discussing the restructuring of the national territories, which would include giving Croatia some political power of its own. The new solution carved-up Bosnia giving some parts to Croatia and leaving other parts to be devoured by Serbia. The Bosnian Muslim leader Spaho died during these negotiations and his successor Džafer Kulenović sought the creation of a separate banate for Bosnia. His requests were ignored as much of the banates not absorbed into the new Croatia banates had a majority Serb population who wanted to maintain close ties with the remaining banates dominated by Serbia.

These debates continued until the pressure asserted from the German Reich became too much to bear for the Yugoslav government. With Hitler on their border and the Italians already in Greece, Prince Paul realized the impossibility of protection from Great Britain and signed the Axis pact in Vienna on March 25, 1941. When the Yugoslav delegation returned, the Prince was ousted in a bloodless coup and a new government of national unity was formed. The new government tried to continue a conciliatory policy towards Germany but ten days later massive bombing raids on Belgrade began, and Yugoslavia was invaded by German, Bulgarian, Hungarian and Italian forces. The 'resistance' lasted eleven days, after which the Yugoslav army surrendered to the German High Command.

The Second World War

After the defeat of the Yugoslav army, Yugoslavia was divided between the Axis powers. Its territories became important for communication and supplies of natural resources and labor to fight the Allied powers. The Axis powers were focused on defeating the Allied forces and were not prepared for the war against the Yugoslav resistance movements, and the two civil wars that ensued.

Before the end of the blitzkrieg the Germans had proclaimed a new 'Independent State of Croatia' (known as NDH), which also engulfed all of Bosnia and Herzegovina. Croatian extremists conducted a war largely against the Serb populations in Croatia and Bosnia and Herzegovina. There was also war between the two main resistance groups – the *četnici*, who were Serbs loyal to the monarchy, and the communist partisans that enlisted Serbs, Muslims and Croats.

Under the leadership of Josip Broz, or Tito, the partisans envisioned a communist victory over the Germans and a social revolution that would create a post-war communist state. Tito was a Stalin loyalist whose revolutionary ideology attracted a population that was weary and worn by nationalist agendas.

Two of the most crucial battles of WWII in Yugoslavia took place in Bosnia and Herzegovina. In the early months of 1943 the most epic battle for the partisans began – the Battle of the Neretva. A surprise counter offensive was launched by the partisans in the direction of Herzegovina and Montenegro. In retreat from battles in the Krajina region the partisans reached the Neretva River with 4,000 wounded and many more villagers who had joined the partisans in fleeing from German attacks. With over 20,000 *četnik* troops on one side and Axis forces on the other, Tito sabotaged the bridge at Jablanica, leading the enemy to believe the partisans had changed course. He ordered the bridge to be destroyed and improvised a wooden footbridge. All the wounded were brought across and the footbridge destroyed, thus deceiving the German forces. The partisans now faced the *četnik* army, and in a fierce battle the *četniks* were wiped out. Tito and the partisans were able to secure a safe passage to Montenegro. The remains of the bridge can still be seen today in Jablanica and there is a full account of the battle at the museum in that town.

By May the Germans had begun preparations for the largest campaign of the war. Over 100,000 troops, backed by air power, surrounded the outnumbered partisans in the mountainous region near the River Sutjeska in eastern Bosnia. The Partisans attempted to break through to the eastern border with Montenegro and over 7,000 partisans lost their lives. Today Sutjeska is a National Park that pays tribute to the downed partisans.

Tito's Yugoslavia

Depending on who you talk to, Tito was either a monstrous communist dictator or a peacekeeping socialist visionary. The truth probably lies somewhere in the middle. At the end of WWII, Yugoslavia, like much of Europe, was a mess. Tito quickly introduced Stalinist methodology in running his new communist republic. His logic was that in order to plant the seeds of socialist ideology, nationalist sentiments must be uprooted and weeded out at all costs. This resulted in the death of what some estimate to be 250,000 Croats, Muslims and Serbs. The Department for the Protection of the People, Tito's secret police, arrested and often severely punished anyone who opposed 'brotherhood and unity', and in fact anyone they *thought* might threaten the new fragile state. The Croats were especially targeted, some having supported the ustaša and been followers of Ante Pavelić.

The Franciscan clergy in Herzegovina were also singled out, having been suspected of supporting the *ustaša* against the Partisans. Many churches were destroyed and monasteries shut down. Serbian *Četniks* were also seriously persecuted and many either left the country or retreated to isolated mountain areas. The Muslims were also served harsh punishments; executions of the Muslim intellectual elite were commonplace in the early years after the war. The courts of Islamic sacred law were suppressed, teaching of children in mosques became a criminal offense, women were forbidden to wear the veil and many Muslim cultural societies were forced to close.

In 1948 Stalin expelled Yugoslavia from the Cominform. At this time Tito quickly changed his platform from being a stark Stalinist to being a more open minded, independent and liberal socialist. By the mid-fifties, religious life in Yugoslavia improved, with new laws that allowed freedom of religion, although the state was mandated with directing and controlling these institutions.

Whereas the first half of the new Yugoslavia was built around establishing authority, rebuilding, and weeding out opposition, Yugoslavia in the 1960s and beyond brought about a kind of national renaissance. It is from this point on that people speak of the glorious days of Tito - when everyone had a job and there was free education. There were no homeless and people were free to travel around the world.

Massive changes to the infrastructure, particularly road systems, opened much of the impenetrable Bosnia and Herzegovina for the first time. The National Roads Launch of 1968 aimed at connecting every town in the country with asphalt roads. Almost a thousand schools and libraries were built. The library program was co-funded by Nobel Laureate Ivo Andrić. He donated half of his prize money for this project. Schools in rural areas and small villages were established as were small medical clinics or 'ambulanta.' The university system was expanded from Sarajevo to Banja Luka, Tuzla, Mostar, Zenica, and other major cities in Bosnia and Herzegovina.

Tito established and maintained good relations with both the United States and the Soviet Union and Yugoslavia received financial aid from both of them in a typical cold war 'tug-o-war.' New incentives by the communist party for 'self-management' within the republics gave the population a sense of pride and independence. For the average person in Bosnia and Herzegovina, life was good. People had jobs, relatively comfortable lifestyles and were free to travel and work abroad.

After Tito

After the death of Tito in 1980, Bosnia and Herzegovina continued to enjoy relative prosperity. The deepening crisis in Kosovo in the early eighties, however, gave further fuel to the Serbian nationalist cause. Dobrica Ćosić, a Serbian nationalist Communist, complained that 'one could witness among the Serbian people a re-ignition of the old historic goal and national idea – the unification of the Serbian people into a single state.' This statement led to his expulsion from the Central Committee. Ćosić also fiercely opposed the granting of national status to the Bosnian Muslims. Anti-Muslim, and for nationalist propaganda purposes, anti-Islamic, sentiment was fuel for the fire of Serbian nationalism.

By the mid-1980s, the economic situation in Yugoslavia began to deteriorate. Without the strong leadership of Tito, poor economic times gave further rise to nationalism. In 1987 inflation rose 120% and by the next year that rate had doubled. In the last few years of the eighties strikes and protests became commonplace. In 1989 strikes against the local party leaders in Vojvodina and Montenegro set the stage for the new leader of the Serbian Communists – Slobodan Milošević.

Milošević clearly had an agenda of transformation in Serbia and he quickly replaced party leaders with his own supporters. In March 1989, at Milošević's request, the Serbian Assembly passed a constitutional amendment that abolished the autonomy of Kosovo and Vojvodina. This was met by massive strikes in Kosovo that were violently dealt with by the Serbian security forces. In a general atmosphere of discontent among the masses, due to the worsening economic times, political finger pointing stirred a nationalist fury that few could have imagined. The Serbs could now either dominate Yugoslavia or break it up. Even at this point, however, few Bosnians saw the rise of nationalism or the deepening economic woes as a sign of war or disintegration. Life, for the most part, carried on as normal.

The break-up of Yugoslavia

The symbolic turning point in the collapse of Yugoslavia came in the summer of 1989 at Kosovo polje. Hundreds of thousands of Serbs gathered at this ancient battle-field to pay respects to Prince Lazar, who had been slain at this place in 1389 in battle against the Ottomans. In the weeks leading up to the ceremony the bones of the Prince toured Serbia, stirring the pot of unsettled scores in the minds of many Serbs. Milošević addressed those assembled saying that 'we are again engaged in battles and quarrels. They are not yet armed battles, but this cannot be ruled out yet.' His words clearly stuck a resounding chord and were met with thundering applause. Through careful nationalist rhetoric Milošević secured half of the eight votes in the federal government. He controlled Serbia, Montenegro, Kosovo and Vojvodina. In his eyes that left only the challenge of getting Macedonia on board to gain a majority and further implement constitutional change in favor of Serbian dominance.

With the fall of the Berlin wall came the unification of East and West Germany and the almost overnight collapse of the Soviet Union. Faced now with a struggling economy and the shift from a planned to a market economy, there were demands by the republics for more freedom and sovereignty from the federal government. The Serbian government attempted to block any movement toward the break-up of Yugoslavia. Talk of independence increased in Slovenia and Croatia in 1990, and at the 14th Congress of the League of Communists of Yugoslavia, President Slobodan Milošević issued a warning that republics seeking independence would face border changes on the assumption that anywhere a Serb lived was part of Serbia. This only fueled Croatian nationalism which had become more radical in the late eighties. As Milošević's power base expanded, the 'dream' of an independent Croatia became increasingly appealing to many Croats.

In Bosnia and Herzegovina, the Serbian propaganda machine shifted its focus from the *ustaša* hordes to the Islamic fundamentalist threat. In reality, Bosnia's Muslim population, especially after almost 50 years of socialism, was mainly secular and pro-Europe. Holding a 44% minority in the country they feared that both Serbian and Croatian lust to take Bosnia and Herzegovina would leave them nation-less.

As was done in Slovenia and Croatia, a referendum for independence was held in Bosnia and Herzegovina in March 1992. The Bosnian Croats and Muslims voted in favor, whilst a majority of the Serbian population boycotted the vote. With sixty-five per cent of Bosnia's population voting in favor, Bosnia and Herzegovina declared independence notwithstanding Serbian threats. The day the results were announced Serb paramilitary forces set up barricades and sniper posts near the parliament building in Sarajevo. Suddenly, the heavy artillery and tanks that had already surrounded Sarajevo and several other cities before the independence vote, were a very real threat.

On April 6, 1992 the European Union and the United Nations recognized Bosnia and Herzegovina as an independent state. On the same day the Yugoslav National Army and Serbian paramilitaries attacked Sarajevo. Tens of thousands of Sarajevans of all nationalities took to the streets to protest in front of the barricades. As the crowd peacefully marched toward the barricade a sniper from the hillside fired into the crowd, killing a woman from Sarajevo and a Muslim woman who had fled the fighting in Dubrovnik. This sparked the beginning of what would be a long and brutal campaign against Bosnia's non-Serb populations.

In less than a year Yugoslavia saw three of its six republics secede. Macedonia followed suit and a UN preventive force was sent to intersect any pending ambitions Serbia had on Macedonia. Serbia and Montenegro, together with the provinces of Vojvodina and Kosovo, were now all that remained of Yugoslavia

The conflict

There have been so many books written about this subject that the authors have decided to let the reader, if they so choose, to further research the conflict. For the sake of sparing this book from the dark days of the early 1990's we will skip the details of the war that flashed on our screens from 1992 to 1995. Although this issue is still a topic of heavy debate here it is clear that Bosnia and Herzegovina experienced the worst genocide on European soil since WWII. Addressing the truths of the war is a necessary process for healing – both by victim and aggressor, but we feel that this is not the place for this. In short, we have moved on from those days and hope our readers will too and fully experience the beauty of Bosnia and Herzegovina today.

What one rarely learns or reads about of conflicts such as this one is the 'other side of the coin.' A spirit of resistance and survival thrived during these times. Communities mobilized to help one another. An untapped strength and creativity was expressed through the war theatre in Sarajevo that put on plays for the duration the siege. The newspaper *Oslobođenje*, meaning Freedom, did not miss a single day of print despite the lack of paper and supplies. Cultural life did not die during these times, it flourished in the most defiant form of non-violent resistance. Bosnians walked through the hail of gunfire to have coffee with a friend and held a Miss Sarajevo beauty pageant in a basement during one of the worst periods of the war. The attempts to erase all material traces of Bosnia's Muslim and Islamic culture may have partially succeeded in the torching of libraries and razing of mosques, but the spirit of a multi-ethnic community never died. Hundreds of thousands of Bosnians – Muslim, Serb and Croat – lost their lives, some in the most horrific ways imaginable. And although in some circles the madness of ethnic purity still exists you will find that in most places in Bosnia today people are determined to live a normal life again, and to live together...as they always have.

Post-war Bosnia and Herzegovina

Difficult times and a long rehabilitation process followed the signing of the Dayton Peace Accords. Although progress and reform has come slow in the eyes of the local inhabitants, great strides have been made in the normalization of life in Bosnia and Herzegovina. In the early years after Dayton the peace was monitored and enforced by a large NATO presence. Sarajevo became the headquarters of the multi-national peacekeeping force and the Brits, Americans and French commanded their respective jurisdictions in the rest of the country with smaller NATO countries under their command. More importantly, electricity, food, and water returned to the beleaguered population. Shops were once again filled with European products and a massive reconstruction program began on a scale not seen since the Marshall Plan.

Freedom of movement between the entities was improved with the introduction of standardized car license plates. Registration plates after the war clearly stated which entity one was from, which often led to harassment and/or random violence. The return of refugees was a slower process and one that is still ongoing. Large numbers of refugees and displaced persons have returned to their rightful homes, but many remain in third countries or internally displaced within Bosnia and Herzegovina.

Government reform was and still is a painful process. The nationalist parties that led the country into war still ruled in the immediate years after Dayton. The new constitution stipulates the full equal rights and representation of all three peoples of Bosnia and Herzegovina, giving even minority groups an unprecedented voice in government. The presidency is not a one-person position but rather a three-person consortium with rotating powers to the Serb, Croat, and Bosniac delegates. The circus of establishing an equally balanced government was no less than a poorly constructed jigsaw puzzle. Ministry positions were given to political parties regardless of the background or competency of the individuals involved. Appointees stuck hard to party lines instead of nation building. Corruption was rampant and became an inherent part of the system, and has proved very difficult to uproot. This did little to improve the power of a centralized government, nor help begin the process of reconciliation.

Bosnia and Herzegovina was assigned an internationally mandated governing body to oversee the rebuilding process, called the Office of the High Representative (OHR). Most Bosnians viewed the NATO forces as peaceful and necessary occupiers and have a similar opinion of the OHR. The powers of the OHR are broad and sweeping, so much so that in essence they play an ad hoc protectorate role. Free and fair elections were implemented by the Office for Security and Cooperation in Europe (OSCE). The elections in 2002 were the first elections to be fully implemented by the local government. Previously elected officials were only able to serve two-year terms that were often counter productive to time consuming reform. The elections of 2002 were the first four-year term mandates in post Dayton Bosnia and Herzegovina. The OHR has embarked on an aggressive campaign to eliminate corruption and bureaucratic overspending. Steps to attract foreign investment have finally been implemented. European standards are being pushed on taxes, environment and transparency.

What this means for the ordinary person here is hope for a stable future. The short-term reality however is a rather corrupt system that lacks a coherent vision of building a united country. Great strides have been made but life in Bosnia and Herzegovina still faces rough economic times, with war criminals still not brought to justice, and many people left to deal on a daily basis with the scars of war. This may not seem so evident to the visitor. The quest for a normal life has in many places created a lively atmosphere. Café's are always full of smiling faces, people walk the streets wearing the finest of European fashions, and the warm hospitality you're sure to find everywhere will certainly make you ask 'Why did this happen here? This is really a great place.' Bosnians ask themselves this question every day.

PRACTICAL INFORMATION

WHEN TO VISIT

For the two co-authors of this book it's very difficult to say when the best time to visit would be - we both live in Bosnia now and we love it all year round. Summer and Spring are the obvious warm seasons with plenty of fun and sun to be had. But winter skiing and the autumn colours are equally nice. People are always out and about in this country - it's certainly one of the most social places we've come across - and you'll never miss the local crowds. You've got the best of both worlds here, Alpine and Mediterranean - enjoy them both, any time of year!

In spring, the country is at its best. So green, so many flowers. The days are pleasantly warm and the evenings are refreshingly cool. In summer time, it is nice and warm in Sarajevo, but sometimes a little too hot (30+ °C) in Mediterranean Herzegovina. Prices for accommodation are generally a little higher in July and August.

If you come to Bosnia and Herzegovina only once, and you are not into winter sports, spring and summer are the best times. But if you come to the country regularly, or if you are into wet walks, autumn is not to be missed. October and November are good months to avoid the crowds and enjoy the barrage of orange, red and yellow leaves that paint the forests. These months see both rainy and cool, sunny days.

Bosnia in general and the mountainous regions in particular have very cold winters and high snow precipitation. If you are a skier, the best time for a visit is from January to March. Olympic skiing on the Bjelašnica, Igman and Jahorina mountains is perfect in these three months. In this period, people from the region flock to these areas. If you plan on coming and you want a hotel close to the ski lifts, it is best to make reservations. And make sure to buy snow chains: the road clearance teams are getting better but the roads in winter are still not quite as good as they would be in other parts of the world.

ENTERING BOSNIA AND HERZEGOVINA

With the right papers, entering Bosnia and Herzegovina is easy. Procedures at both the borders and the airport are standardized and uncomplicated. Only during the holiday season, when the people living in the Diaspora flock into the country, do border crossings sometimes take a bit of time.

Bosnia and Herzegovina can only be entered with a valid passport. EU, American and Canadian citizens do not require a visa to enter the country. Most other people do need a visa, and getting one is difficult. Visas are issued by the country's diplomatic missions. Visas for private travel require an application form and a letter of intent from somebody who resides in Bosnia and Herzegovina. Business visas require an application form, an invitation from an in-country business partner and a letter of intent from the Bosnia and Herzegovina Trade Office. Visa applicants from certain countries should also provide evidence of possession of cash assets, as well as HIV test results.

Fees for visas issued by diplomatic/consular offices:

Single entry-exit visas and transit visas	31.00 KM
Multiple entry-exit visas for periods up to 90 days	57.00 KM
Multiple entry-exit visa for periods over 90 days	72.00 KM

Officially, people who enter the country on a visa need to register themselves with the police within 24 hours after their arrival in the country. Any violation of this regulation could officially entail a financial penalty or even deportation. In reality, I have frequently received visitors who required a visa to enter, I never registered any of them and none of them ever ran into any type of problem as a consequence. Similarly, you might be asked to fill in a card upon arrival in Sarajevo Airport – but at the time of writing this card was no longer being distributed.

If you enter Bosnia and Herzegovina by car, you will have to buy vehicle insurance at the border. It is an uncomplicated and fairly inexpensive affair. You do not need this insurance if you have a green card that covers Bosnia and Herzegovina (something that is not normally the case).

Both local alcoholic beverages and cigarettes are relatively cheap in Bosnia and Herzegovina, and the only money you could save would be on brand-name alcohol. You are allowed to import 200 cigarettes and 2 liters of liquor.

DIPLOMATIC MISSIONS

Bosnia and Herzegovina embassies overseas

Australia:	5 Beale Crescent, Deakin, ACT 2600 Canberra; tel: +61 2 6232 4646; fax: +61 2 6232 55 54
Austria:	Tivoligasse 54, A-1120 Wien; tel: +43 1 810 1252; fax: +43 1 811 8569
Belgium:	Rue Tenbosch 34, 1000 Bruxelles; tel: +32 2 644 2008; fax: +32 2 644 1698
Canada:	130 Albert St, Suite 805, Ottawa, Ontario K1P 5G4; tel: +1 613 236 0028; fax: +1 613 236 1139
Croatia:	Torbarova 9, Zagreb 10000; tel: +385 1 468 3761; fax: +385 1 468 3764

Denmark: Nytory 3, 1450 Copenhagen K; tel: +45 33 33 80 40;
              fax: +45 33 33 80 17
France: 174 rue de Courcelles, 75017 Paris;
              tel: +33 1 42 67 34 22; fax: +33 1 40 53 85 22
Germany: Ibsenstrasse 14, D-10439 Berlin; tel: +49 30 814 712
              10; fax: +49 30 814 712 11
Greece: Hatzikosta 3, 11521 Atena; tel: +30 210 64 11 375;
              fax: +30 210 64 23 154
Hungary: Pasareti śt 48, 1026 Budapest; tel: +36 1 212 0106;
              fax: +36 1 212 0109
Italy: Via Fabio Filzi 19, Milano; tel: +39 02 669 82 707;
              fax: +39 02 669 81 467
The Netherlands: Bezuidenhoutseweg 223, 2594 AL, The Hague;
              tel: +31 70 35 88 505; fax: +31 70 35 84 367
Norway: Bygday Alle 10, 0262 Oslo; tel: +47 22 54 09 63;
              fax: +47 22 55 27 50
Serbia and Montenegro: Milana Tankošića 8, 11 000 Belgrade;
              tel: +381 11 329 1277
Slovenia: Kalarjeva 26, 1000 Ljubljana; tel: +386 1 432 4042;
              fax: +386 1 432 2230
Spain: Calle Lagasca 24.2, Izda, 28001 Madrid;
              tel: +349 1 575 08 70; fax: +349 1 435 50 56
Switzerland: Jungfraustrasse 1, CH-3005 Bern;
              tel: +41 31 351 1051; fax: +41 31 351 1079
Sweden: Birger Jarisgaten 55/3, 11145 Stockholm;
              tel: +468 44 00 540; +468 24 98 30
Turkey: Turan Emeksiz Sokak 3, Park Siteler 9/3,
              Gaziomanpasa, Ankara; tel: +90 312 427 3602;
              fax: +90 312 427 3604
United Kingdom: 5-7 Lexan Gardens, London W8 5JJ;
              tel: +44 20 7373 0867; fax: +44 20 7373 0871
United States of America: 2109 E St NW, Washington DC 20037;
              tel: +1 202 337 1500; fax: +1 202 337 1502

Foreign embassies in Bosnia and Herzegovina

The country code is +387. All embassies are in Sarajevo. The postcode for
Sarajevo is 71000.

Austria: Džidžikovac 7; tel: 033 668 337; fax: 033 668 339
Bulgaria: Soukbunar 15; tel: 033 668 191; fax: 033 668 182
Canada: Grbavička 4/2; tel: 033 222 033, 033 447 901;
              fax: 033 222 004
China: Braće Begić 17; 033 215 102; fax: 033 215 108
Croatia: Mehmeda Spahe 16; tel: 033 444 330/1;
              fax: 033 472 434;
              Consular Section: Skenderija 17; 033 442 591;
              fax: 033 650 328

Czech Republic: Franjevačka 19; tel: 033 447 525, 033 446 966;
fax: 033 447 526

Denmark: Splitska 9; tel: 033 665 901; fax: 033 665 902

Egypt: Nurudina Gackića 58; tel: 033 666 498;
fax: 033 666 499

France: Mehmed-bega Kapetanovića Ljubušaka 18;
tel: 033 668 149, 033 668 151; fax: 033 212 186

Germany: Mejtaš-Buka 11-13; tel: 033 275 000, 033 275 080;
fax: 033 652 978, 033 443 176

Greece: Obala Maka Dizdara 1; tel: 033 213 439;
fax: 033 203 512

Hungary: Hasana Bibera 53; tel: 033 205 302;
fax: 033 268 930;
Consular Section: Safet-bega Bašagića 58a

Iran: Obala Maka Dizdara 6; tel: 033 650 210;
fax: 033 663 910

Italy: Čekaluša 39; tel: 033 203 959; fax: 033 659 368

Japan: Mula Mustafe Bašeskije 2; tel: 033 209 580;
fax: 033 209 583

Libya: Tahtali sokak 17; tel: 033 200 621; fax: 033 663 620

Macedonia: Emerika Bluma 23; tel: 033 269 402, 033 206 004;
fax: 033 206 004

Malaysia: Trnovska 6; tel: 033 201 578; fax: 033 667 713

Malta: Mula Mustafe Bašeskije 12; tel: 033 668 632;
fax: 033 668 632

Netherlands: Grbavička 4, I sprat; tel: 033 223 404, 033 223 410;
fax: 033 223 413

Norway: Ferhadija 20; tel: 033 254 000; fax: 033 666 505

Pakistan: Emerika Bluma 17; tel: 033 211 836;
fax: 033 211 837

Palestine: Čemerlina 4; tel: 033 272 700/1; fax: 033 238 677

Poland: Dola 13; tel: 033 201 142; fax: 033 233 796

Portugal: Čobanija 12; tel: 033 200 835; fax: 033 443 117

Romania: Tahtali sokak 13-15; tel: 033 207 447;
fax: 033 668 940

Russia: Urijan Dedina 93-95; tel: 033 668 147;
fax: 033 668 148

Saudi Arabia: Koševo 44; tel: 033 211 861; fax: 033 212 204

Slovenia: Bentbaša 7; tel: 033 271 260; fax: 033 271 270

Spain: Čekaluša 16; tel: 033 278 560; fax: 033 278 582

Serbia and Montenegro: Obala Maka Dizdara 3a; tel: 033 260 080;
fax: 033 221 469

Sweden: Ferhadija 20; tel: 033 276 030; fax: 033 276 060

Switzerland: Josipa Štadlera 15; tel: 033 275 850;
fax: 033 665 246

Turkey: Hamdije Kreševljakovića 5; tel: 033 445 260;
fax: 033 443 190

United Kingdom: Tina Ujevića 8; tel: 033 282 200;
              fax: 033 666 131;
              Consular Section: Petrakijina 11; tel: 033 208 229;
              fax: 033 204 780
United States of America: Alipašina 43; tel: 033 445 700;
              fax: 033 659 722
Vatican: Pehlivanuša 9; tel: 033 207 847; fax: 033 207 863

In Mostar

Office of United States of America: Mostarskog bataljona bb;
              tel: 036 580 580
Consulate of Republic Croatia: Zagrebačka 8; tel: 036 316 630
General Consulate of Republic Turkey: Mala Tepa 24;
              tel: 036 551 209

In Banja Luka

Austria: Jovana Dučića 52; tel: 051 311 144
Croatia: Milana Karanovića 1; tel: 051 304 258
Germany and France: DR.M.Stojanovića 1; tel: 051 303 925
United Kingdom: Simeuna Đaka 8; tel: 051 216 843
United States of America: Jovana Dučića 5; tel: 051 221 590

GETTING THERE AND AWAY

Bosnia and Herzegovina has a well-connected capital. It is easily accessible by air, bus, or train. The airport is only 20 minutes away from the city centre and has direct flights to many European capitals and thus indirect flights to everywhere else. Many local and international bus lines depart from the centre of town. The train schedule is less extensive, but does offer a few really good trips in comfortable trains at very modest prices.

By air

The state-of-the-art Sarajevo airport (033 289 100) is located at the base of Mount Igman. In winter, this is probably the worst possible location for an airport in Sarajevo and surroundings. In the cold months, early-morning flights are regularly cancelled as the entire area is often covered with heavy fog until late morning or later. In all other seasons, this airport is a pleasure to arrive at and depart from.

The airport is 12 km from the town centre. There are no shuttle buses and no bus routes in the vicinity of the airport. At various rates, the major hotels - and some of the smaller ones - offer airport pick-ups and drop-offs. Otherwise, taxis will take you to town for either the meter fee or a fixed amount of 20 KM.

You can change money at the airport exchange desk, rent a car from one of the car rental boots located in the arrival hall, and, in case you need to contact your hotel, buy a phone card at the post office. If your luggage did not arrive, you have to register the missing suitcases at the lost and found office, located next to the coffee shop in the arrival hall.

As Bosnia and Herzegovina is neither a main destination nor a major hub, flights to Sarajevo are relatively costly. The most affordable tickets used to come from the official airline of Bosnia and Herzegovina - Air Bosna – but this airline recently went bankrupt. Depending on the season, a return ticket from London will cost between £200 and £400. From most Euro countries a ticket will costs between 250 and 450 Euro, and from New York it will be between $700 and a little over $1,000. At the time of writing, ten international carriers have regular flights to and from Sarajevo:

Adria Airways:	Ferhadija 23/II; tel: 033 289 245 (airport), 033 232 125/6; fax: 033 233 692
Avio Express Airlines:	Zelenih beretki 22; tel: 033 653 179; fax: 033 208 334
Austrian Airlines:	Maršala Tita 54; tel: 033 474 445 (airport), 033 474 446/7; fax: 033 470 526
Croatia Airlines:	Kranjčevićeva 4/1a; tel: 033 258 600 (airport), 033 666 123; fax: 033 463 158
Lufthansa:	Alipašina bb; tel: 033 474 445 (airport), 033 278 590/1/2
Turkish Airlines:	Kulovića 5; tel: 033 289 249 (airport), 033 666 092; 033 212 938
Malev:	Kurta Schorka 36; tel: 033 289 246 (airport), 033 473 200/1; fax: 033 467 105
JAT:	Zelenih beretki 6; tel: 033 259 750 (airport), 033 259 750/1; fax: 033 223 083

Sometimes, it is cheaper to buy your tickets from a travel agency. The cheapest and most reliable ticket agent in Sarajevo is Kompas Travel in the city centre (Maršala Tita 8; tel: 033 208 014; fax: 033 208 015; email: kompas@kompas-sarajevo.com; web: www.kompas-sarajevo.com). A comprehensive overview of all other travel agencies is available at the Sarajevo Old Town Tourist Information Office.

There are international airports in Mostar, Tuzla and Banja Luka as well.

By ferry

Bosnia and Herzegovina has only one tiny strip of coast at Neum and there are no ferries that dock there. With seasonal schedules, ferries do come from Italy (Ancona and Bari) to the ports of Split and Dubrovnik. If you are traveling by car, these ferries may save you traffic jams along the Croatian coast. If you do not have your own means of transport, you will find the transfer to the bus stations at the port (in Split) or close to it (in Dubrovnik) easy and hassle-free. If you are a ferry person, check the ferry companies websites: SEM (www.sem-marina.hr), Jadrolinija (www.jadrolinija.hr) and Adriatica Navigazione (www.adriatica.it).

By rail

Buses drive fast, use curvy roads and confine you to your chair from beginning to end. Getting around by train is a little slower, but much more comfortable. In Bosnia and Herzegovina, trains are punctual, low-cost, and sometimes fairly luxurious, with couches that can be turned into beds, and cabins that are very often completely empty.

Before the war the rail network connected most Bosnian cities. This has changed dramatically. There are now only three routes that originate in Sarajevo: the Sarajevo-Zenica-Banja Luka-Zagreb route takes about ten hours from start to finish; the northern route to Budapest goes via Tuzla; and the southern route towards the Adriatic coast is Konjic-Jablanica-Mostar-Čapljina-Ploče (Ploče is in Croatia). This last route goes through the Neretva Canyon and is particularly scenic. Even on these three routes, trains do not go quite as frequently as the buses do.

Daily trains to and from Sarajevo

	To	From	cost (KM)	duration
Budapest	20.20	18.30	92/180	13 hours
Ploče	06.20/18.40	05.00/13.30	18/29	5 hours
Zagreb	09.49	09.00	45/74	9 hours

Recently, Bosnia and Herzegovina joined the Eurorail system. Perhaps that will fill up these sadly empty trains a bit more.

By bus

The bus system of Bosnia and Herzegovina functions well. Centrotrans and a range of smaller bus companies have reliable bus routes to and from all towns and many villages. Every city and town has a bus station with the daily departure and arrival times posted in local language on the station's wall. Ask the people behind the counters if the schedule is not clear to you: they are not likely to speak English (though in Sarajevo they often do) but will point you in the right direction. Asking a person who is standing around waiting is also a good way of double-checking that you are getting on the right bus. People are very willing to help.

Bus travel is reasonably priced and a one-way ticket to the furthest in-country destination from Sarajevo will not cost more than 30 KM. At the smaller stations, you pay when you get on the bus. At the main bus stations, you are meant to buy your ticket at the ticket booth, but even there you can normally get it on the bus as well. Usually there is an extra charge of 1 or 2 KM for each sizeable bag you carry with you. Bus stations do not have lockers or temporary luggage storage places.

Longer trips have breaks, the frequency and duration of which depending on whether or not the driver smokes. In addition, bus drivers may have special deals with restaurants en route. If so, the breaks will be longer to encourage you to eat and drink.

You might want to check out the bus before you get on. Most buses are comfortable and clean but there is the occasional company that has ratty buses with broken seats, windows that don't open, no air conditioning and a driver who smokes the entire length of the journey.

Useful terms

place of departure	mjesto odlaska
destination	destinacija
day of trip	dan vožnje (Pon-Mon, Uto-Tue, Sri-Wed, Čet-Thu, Pet-Fri, Sub-Sat, Ned-Sun)
time of departure	vrijeme odlaska
search	pretraga
departure	odlazak
arrival	dolazak
duration	trajanje
price	cijena

Centrotrans is a Eurolines member and runs regular buses from many European destinations to Sarajevo. Bus schedules, on-line reservations and main European office addresses can be found on the Centrotrans website: www.centrotrans.com. At the time of writing, the Centrotrans schedule is as follows:

From	Days	Single (KM/Euros)	Return (KM/Euros)
Amsterdam	Wed, Sat	250/127	370/188
Antwerp	Wed	230/114	330/165
Berlin	Sat	225/115	325/115
Dortmund	Mon, Tue, Thu, Fri, Sat	239/122	358/183
Dubrovnik	every day	40/20.50	60/ 30.5
Hamburg	Fri	239/122	358/183
Ljubljana	Mon, Wed, Fri	70/36	120/ 61
Makarska	every day	27/14	38/ 19.5
Munich	every day	102/52	141/ 72
Pula	Mon, Wed, Fri, Sat	80/41	130/ 66.5
Rotterdam	Sun,Thu	240/122	340/174
Stuttgart	Sun	156/80	235/120
Split	every day	30/15.50	45/ 23
Vienna	every day	72/37	115/ 59
Zagreb	every day	50/25.50	80 / 41

By car

If you are in a hurry to get from A to B, Bosnia and Herzegovina is not the ideal place to be. There are no real highways and there is not much scope for high-speed driving as roads tend to wind through river valleys and up-and downhill. However, if you are not in any particular hurry, driving from town to town in Bosnia and Herzegovina is as pleasant as driving gets. There is lots of beautiful scenery, the roads tend to be quiet, and there are plenty of quality places to stop for a drink or a meal. Strangely, some of the country's best restaurants are right next to a major road. There is little chance of running out of petrol in the middle of nowhere as there are many petrol stations pretty much everywhere. Equally comforting is the number of garages. For relatively little money and almost always right away, the 'automehaničar' will make repairs and the 'vulkanizer' will fix your flat tire.

Driving in Bosnia and Herzegovina is nice, but some warnings are in order:

- The first few times you go through them, the tunnels of Bosnia and Herzegovina are unnerving. They are unlit and entering them on a sunny day is blinding. Your eyes will need a few seconds to adjust to the pitch black. You cannot just assume that straight driving will be safe as tunnels may curve and may have pot-holes and water dripping from the ceiling. Most tunnels have a sign indicating the length of the tunnel to prepare you for what is in store. Don't forget to take off your sunglasses before entering! I forgot it once and will never forget the experience.

- Take a good map with you. Road signs in some areas are frequent and accurate but they may suddenly be gone altogether.

- Road signs in the Republika Srpska are mostly in Cyrillic. There is a Cyrillic alphabet section in the back of this book.

- First-hand and second-hand spare parts for German-made cars are widely available. For other cars, spare parts may be a little more difficult to find.

- People might tell you that fuel is best bought in the Federation, as some stations in the Republika Srpska have a reputation for mixing water in with the fuel. I have never had any trouble myself.

- The law stipulates that you always have to carry a spare tyre, a jack, an extra headlight bulb, a first-aid kit, a tow rope and a hazard triangle. During a routine police check you may have to show that you do indeed have all that.

- In the winter period, snow chains are vital.

It takes three hours to reach Sarajevo from the border at Metković/Doljani in southern Dalmatia. The route going through Trebinje and Stolac takes one hour more, but nonetheless has my personal preference every time I go to Dubrovnik, as the route is scenic and quiet. From the Split area the best route goes through Kamensko, Livno, Bugojno and Travnik. The route through Tomislav-Grad to Jablanica is stunning, but much of the road is not asphalted, and there are a few forks without signs. There is a road from Sinj via Bili Brig to Livno as well. It may look tempting on the map but is all but inaccessible in reality. From the north, the quickest route to Sarajevo is from Slavonski Brod and Bosanski Brod. However, this route is *not* advisable if this is your first trip to the country. The reason is the war damage you'll see along the road between Brod and Doboj. With every single house completely destroyed for kilometers on stretch, this is perhaps the most depressing road in the country. The routes going through Bihać or Banja Luka are longer but do not look so awful.

Renting a car is easy but costly. Daily rate vary from 75KM to 150KM (with occasional offers at lower prices), with discounts offered if you rent for a longer period. All major cities have car-rental companies. If you arrive at the Sarajevo airport you will find several rental places at the airport. F Rent a Car SA (Kranjčevićeva 39; tel: +387 33 219 177; email: fracsa@team.ba; web: www.frac.co.ba) does airport pick-ups and offers some of the best rates in town, but occasionally fails to give you the car they promised. Avis (tel: +387 33 463 598; fax: +387 33 523 030), Budget (+387 33 234 842 ext. 216), Europcar (tel: +387 33 289 273; fax: +387 33 460 737; email: asa-rent@bih.net.ba) and Hertz (tel: +387 33 668 186) all have desks at the airport. It's usually not a problem to rent a car without reservations when you arrive. Local information on many of the major car-rental companies can be found via links from the international websites and international toll-free phone numbers. Budget offers automatic transmission cars.

Hitchhiking

Unlike hitchhiking in Western Europe, hitchhiking in Bosnia and Herzegovina is not a thing for young people only. On the contrary: many hitchhikers appear to be well over 60.

In the rural areas of Bosnia and Herzegovina, hitchhiking is common practice. In and around the bigger cities it is slightly less common, but there, too, long waits are the exception. Young women rarely hitchhike alone. As in other countries: don't get in if you don't trust the driver.

By bicycle

Roads are often rather narrow and road biking is rare. With the many fast and reckless drivers, biking is not altogether safe on the main routes. But certain parts of the country are just perfect for biking. You can bike for hours on end without experiencing much traffic at all in Popovo polje from Stolac towards Trebinje, or in the large, picturesque valleys of Livanjsko and the Glamočko fields in western Bosnia.

Mountain biking is better still. Hundreds of highland villages are connected by good gravel roads almost everywhere in the country. Igman-Bjelašnica-Visočica in the Sarajevo area offers days of mountain biking trails in breathtaking mountain landscapes.

Bikers should follow the same safety precautions as hikers and stick to the roads and marked paths. Don't wander if you don't know where you are and where you are going. Roads have been cleared of mines, even the isolated gravel ones, but in some places a mine could be just 10m off the side of the road. If you don't know, don't go – or go with a guide.

Hiking

It is already obvious within town: the people from Bosnia and Herzegovina like walking. The habit of taking the car for whatever errand does not exist here, and leisure time with friends or family is often spent on foot, with long strolls through town or in the park. Municipal authorities respect this hobby, and most towns have designated areas for pedestrians only.

And they don't only stroll: all age groups hike, and the hikes they make are often so heavy that the average foreigner will be unable to keep up. These hikes are made for fun – though they can easily take you from town to town and end in family visits - and the routes chosen are beautiful. Deep canyons, raging rivers, high Dinaric peaks, endemic flowers and plants and breathtaking views wherever you turn. For good reasons, big roads are avoided. Pavements do not exist in between towns, road shoulders are rare, and drivers have little respect for pedestrians.

The former Yugoslavia had one of the best-developed systems of mountain trails in Europe. The 'transverzala' connected the Slovenian Alps with the mountains in Macedonia - these trails went through the heart of Bosnia and Herzegovina. Due to the war many trails have disappeared, but mountain associations are in the process of restoring them. The trails' marks are red circles with white dots in the middle. Seeing one is a good sign that you are on a trail that eventually leads to somewhere. You may find the marks on trees or large stones along the trail. The best marked mountain with trail maps is Bjelašnica. The mountain association sells maps and has done an excellent job of keeping the trails clearly marked.

As said repeatedly before, it is not advisable to walk or hike without first checking the mine situation. If you are on a trail that has obviously not been trekked for some time or has faded trail markings you may not want to be there. Fresh trail markings mean that the mountain associations have had the area checked and that they trek it themselves. It is wise to bring a map, compass and GPS if you have one. Check out the sections on safety and what to take for a few additional notes on hiking and hiking requirements.

If you are into hiking, you might want to buy another book of this series. 'Forgotten Beauty' by Matias Gomes describes all hikes over 2,000 meters throughout the country. Without such a book, even the most experienced hiker is recommended to go with a guide. There are literally hundreds of safe trails to trek and hike on. Best not to do it alone.

TOURIST INFORMATION

There are plans to establish a few Bosnia and Herzegovina tourist offices abroad, but at the time of writing none of them had yet opened its doors. The embassies have little or no tourist information available.

Once you are in Sarajevo, the situation is much better. There is a very good tourist information office located close to the cathedral. (tel: 033 220 721/724; fax: 033 532 281; email: tour.off@bih.net.ba; web: www.sarajevo-tourism.com; stand with your back to the cathedral and walk straight down the walkway past Central Café; turn left on Zelene beretke and look for number 22a, 50m down on the right-hand side). Information on hotels, museums, excursions, city tours and other activities is all readily available, and their maps and leaflets are for free. The staff speak English, German,

French and Turkish. They appear to enjoy their work and will go out of their way to help. The very same people give superb guided tours through town.

Alternatively, you could simply check www.city.ba, an up-to-date website on events in the city. The International Women's Club of Sarajevo has produced a well-made practical 'mini' guide to Sarajevo called Opening Doors to Sarajevo, a Selected Guide. The guide is worth the 10KM it costs. Part of the money goes to a good cause.

There is a reasonable tourism information office close to the old bridge in Mostar as well (tel: 036 580 833; email: info@touristinfomostar.co.ba; web: www.touristinfomostar.co.ba).

MAPS

Good road maps of Bosnia and Herzegovina are available in most travel shops, bookshops and airports around Europe. Due to Croatia's odd shape, most maps of Croatia include all of Bosnia and Herzegovina. In-country, maps can be found at a few petrol stations and in some of the bookshops.

All updated European maps include Bosnia and Herzegovina and its main communication arteries. They lack detail and will make you lose your way. The routes suggested by web-based route finders are OK, but the maps are too vague and the estimated travel times do not make any sense at all as the route finders assume unrealistically high average speeds.

The Freytag and Berndt map of Bosnia and Herzegovina and Europe (1:250,000), the Studio FMB map (1:300,000) and the Trasat Polo map of Bosnia and Herzegovina, Croatia and Slovenia (1:500,000) are all good and cost in the range of 12-16 KM. Maps can also be found at www.kakarigi.net/maps (hundreds of maps of cities, towns, mountains and lakes but no map of the country as a whole), www.mapabih.com (for business people) and www.embassyworld.com/maps (lots of links to all sorts of maps). The maps that are available, free of charge, from tourism information centers around the country show the main routes only. If you are really, really into maps, you might want to buy Povijesni Atlas Bosne i Hercegovine, a book with 350 pages of historic maps. At the time of writing, it exists in the local language only, but there are plans to translate it into English.

HEALTH

The chance of getting one of the standard travelers' diseases is very slight, as drinking water throughout the country is excellent and food hygiene is good. Bosnia and Herzegovina has no legal requirements for vaccinations, but visitors are generally advised to be immunized against hepatitis A and B, tetanus, diphtheria, polio, and typhoid. Note that many people ignore this, and that I have never heard of anybody getting sick as a consequence.

To find a pharmacy, ask for 'apoteka'. In major centers, there are many of them, and there is usually at least one that is open 24 hours a day. These pharmacies will generally have all regular prescription drugs readily available. In villages and smaller towns, you may not find a pharmacy at all. If you do find one, it may not stock what you need. The best pharmacy in the country is probably Sarajevo Pharmacy at Saliha Hadžihuseinovića

Muvekita 11 in Sarajevo (tel: 033 722 666; fax: 033 722 667; email: apoteke@bih.net.ba; web: www.apoteke-sarajevo.com).

Public health clinics in Bosnia and Herzegovina are not what they should be, but there are some very good doctors in most towns. It is best to contact your embassy if you need medical attention, as embassies usually have lists of doctors they have good experiences with.

SAFETY

You are going to Bosnia? Are you sure? Why would you do that? Is it safe there? Aren't there mines?

You can't come to Bosnia and Herzegovina without having this conversation. It is an understandable concern: there *are* mines in Bosnia and Herzegovina and, with the clearing process progressing slowly, there will continue to be mines for the decades to come. But that does not mean that visiting Bosnia and Herzegovina is unsafe. So far, no visitor to Bosnia and Herzegovina has ever been involved in a mine incident.

Mine safety is a matter of respecting a few rules:

- Highly populated areas, national parks and conservation areas are all clear of mines and safe to visit.

- Stay away from taped areas. Whether in yellow or red, whether the markings are new or old: just simply never go there.

- If you are in the countryside, stay away from areas that are not obviously frequented by people. Look for cut grass, tire tracks, footprints or rubbish – all indications of safe areas. Obviously, areas in which people are walking, jogging, BBQ-ing et cetera are safe. Conversely, abandoned villages – however much fun it seems to explore them - may pose a threat.

- The most dangerous areas are the former lines of confrontation in the countryside. Many mountain ranges and some rural areas are still contaminated. As tourists and travelers would not normally know much about the location of these former confrontation lines, it is best to take a guide or a local who knows the terrain. Mountain associations and eco-tourism organizations are your best bet for a safe mountain adventure. There is plenty of safe hiking, walking, wandering and exploring to be done in Bosnia and Herzegovina – it is simply not wise to do it alone.

For more information, you could visit the Mine Action Centre (MAC; Zmaja od Bosne 8 in Sarajevo) or visit the center's website (www.bhmac.org).

Apart from the mines, Bosnia and Herzegovina is one of the safest places in Europe. Violent crime is virtually non-existent. For men and women alike, walking the streets of any town or city at any time of day or night is a relatively safe bet.

Traffic may be risky. Most of Bosnia and Herzegovina's roads are narrow and curvy. Road maintenance is getting better but don't let a pot-hole surprise you. The locals tend to drive fast and have little fear of overtaking on a solid line. Other than that, the main concerns for travelers are car thieves and pickpockets. Always lock your car doors, and engage your alarm if you have one. In trams and buses, keep your purse closed and your wallet in your front pocket. Pickpockets are quick and talented, and you will not even know that you have been had until later. They usually work in pairs.

Mountain safety

Bringing a few extras on your hikes adds weight but could save your life in an emergency situation. It is always good to bring high-energy food items. Even outside the summer months a hat and 15+ sunscreen are essential in the mountains. The high mountain sun exposure can be particularly dangerous in summer and a sunstroke is a bad thing to get when you are hours away from help. To prevent sunstroke, also protect your face and back of the neck when the sun is particularly fierce.

Bring water, but also try the sources you'll find on your way. Most water sources are perfectly safe for drinking. Stay away if a source is clogged with moss and algae. Mountain huts on spots without sources closeby generally have water storage reservoirs. If you come across a metal lid near a hut it is probably a rain collection tank. Check it first, but they are usually good for drinking.

Bosnia and Herzegovina is a mountainous land and each valley and range has its own unique system. A rainy day in town could coincide with a sunny afternoon on the mountains around it and freezing winds on their peaks. A consequence is that the weather conditions in town should not affect your packing. The high altitude mountain ranges can experience drastic temperature changes. When a storm or fog rolls in, the temperature can easily drop 10-15° C in a matter of hours. Consequently, even if it is pleasantly warm in town, a warm fleece and an extra shirt and socks could help prevent catching a cold in the mountains.

Many trails are not as well-maintained as they were before the war, so it is best to wear good boots that give you adequate ankle support. Loose rocks, fallen tree limbs or erosion can be enough to twist an ankle and abruptly end your hike.

There are two types of poisonous snakes in Bosnia and Herzegovina. Although their bites are rarely fatal, your first aid box should contain a snake bite kit. These kits can be purchased in most outdoor shops in the West. They are compact, easy to carry, and normally come with very clear instructions. Prevention, of course, is the best protection. Be aware of where you are stepping. In the summer months snakes can be found in clear water rivers and streams. They will also gather on the sunny side of mountains. Be careful around rocky areas with cracks and holes; these are snakes' favorite hiding spots. In the early autumn they tend to linger on tree limbs. The colder air makes them rather lethargic and they are less of a threat than during the hot season. Poisonous snakes only inject venom 25% of the time. If you are bitten it is best to stay calm. The faster your blood circulates the faster the poison travels through your system. Don't let this information scare you. Snakes are more afraid of you than you are of them, and anxious to get out of your way.

Lightning strikes occur frequently on high ridges during a storm, particularly above river canyons. If you see lightning while you are trekking on a ridge get out of there quickly. There are often signs (such as struck-down black pines) that indicate you're in a dangerous area.

It is good practice to let someone know if you plan to hike solo. If you are going with a guide, safety precautions have probably been taken – but it might be wise to check. A mountain rescue service (Gorska služba za spašavanje - GSS) exists but is not present in every region. Rescuers do not always have access to helicopter assistance and it may take some time to reach you in case of an emergency.

WHAT TO TAKE

Almost anything can be bought in Bosnia and Herzegovina, and most items are relatively inexpensive.

In addition to the usual, you might want to take:

- An international driving license if you are not from the surrounding or EU countries.
- Adapters for UK or American plugs. These adapters are not for sale in Bosnia and Herzegovina. The country uses the standard European size and shape (220V and 50Hz) with twin round-pin plugs.
- Sunglasses. Summers are bright, spring and autumn have plenty of bright days, and the reflection of the sun off the snow in winter is blinding.
- A light pair of slippers if you plan on staying with Bosnians or in private accommodation. Most homes have extra slippers, called papuče, but I always find it nice to have my own.
- A jumper. Spring and autumn are similar in that many days are warm and sunny but evenings are chilly. The air is very refreshing but not if you're not dressed adequately. Even on the hottest days in the summer, evenings can be cool.
- The right footwear. The beaches are rocky and full of pebbles, walks require comfortable walking shoes or more, and even in the midst of town many pavements are covered with ice and dirty, cold slush in winter.
- Good winter gear. Thermal underwear, gloves, hat, scarf and rain gear are recommended.

If you intend to hike, you should not forget:

- A water bottle, to be filled at the many springs that you'll pass by on your walks.
- A sunhat, especially if you are planning to do high mountain hikes.
- A snake-bite suction kit, as it's better to be safe than sorry.
- Very sturdy mountain shoes or boots, as many of the trails are not well maintained and loose rocks or roots could cause a serious ankle injury.
- A warm fleece, light rain gear, walking sticks if you use them, and a comfortable rucksack.

- Camping gear, although some of the campsites in Bosnia and Herzegovina provide tents, mats and even sleeping bags.
- Good waterproof gear (gaiters, poncho, waterproof trousers, a protective coat on your shoes) is a good idea if you visit the country in any season other than mid-summer.

Two warnings:

- Winter hiking in this country is an amazing experience, but be prepared for more than 1m of snow above the 1,000m mark during the coldest months. Bring whatever waterproof gear you have. Warm fleeces and thermals are a must. If you plan to hike to over 2,000m, boots that can be worn with crampons are best. If you don't have such gear, you could rent it from a local eco-tourism operator.
- Many travelers find it cool to dress down. Bosnia and Herzegovina is not the country for that. People tend to dress casually, even in fancy places, but their casual clothing matches and is clean and refined. In general, people attach importance to appearance

MEDIA

In the war years, television and radio stations functioned as propaganda machines. There were three main stations, each with limited reach. In addition, there were many dozens of small broadcasters, often focusing on not more than a single municipality. A few years ago, each of these stations was scrutinized and many were closed down. Although many small broadcasters still exist, if only for a few hours per week, most people in Bosnia and Herzegovina have by now moved to one of the larger stations.

There are three main television stations. Luckily for foreign viewers, none of them dubs English language programs. The Federation television station (FTV) and its Republika Srpska counterpart (RTRS) are the two stations envisioned by the Dayton Peace Agreement. They air foreign movies, news, documentaries, music specials and soaps. The best independent station is the Sarajevo-based Hayat. On air 24 hours a day for the people in Bosnia and Herzegovina and for the large diaspora in Europe and North America, Hayat broadcasts local and foreign movies and series, local news, talk shows and documentaries from all over the world. Hayat produces programs as well, for its own use and, on occasion, for CNN. Refreshingly, Hayat does not limit itself to bad news, and managed to give Bosnia and Herzegovina a bit of positive coverage through CNN.

Bosnia Daily is the only English language newspaper in Bosnia and Herzegovina. It is available by electronic subscription only (www.bosniadaily.co.ba; bdaily@megatel.ba). Most subscribers are members of the international community in Bosnia and Herzegovina, and the daily's very strong focus on the role and activities of the international community is therefore logical - but nonetheless somewhat annoying for the outsider. Other than that, this is a relatively good newspaper that carries interesting articles in surprisingly good English.

Apart from Bosnia Daily, all newspapers and magazines are printed in the local language. Perhaps more than anywhere else in the world, the written press feels that bad news sells better than good news, and tends to look very critically at whatever they see around. Endless training from the British and the Americans – through BBC and IREX – have not changed the media's inclination to criticize anything and everything. Going through the local language newspapers, one gets the wrong impression that there is no progress and no hope of progress in this country.

COMMUNICATIONS

Post

Letters to a home address tend to arrive but may take a long time. Packages are a bit riskier and collecting them can be time-consuming. You will receive a yellow slip at the place you are staying, indicating a period within which you should collect your package. With this yellow slip and an ID, you have to come to the post office and go through quite some form-filling and fee-paying. Do not be surprised if your package looks opened and tattered.

There appears to be no service standards and the post office experience depends entirely on the individuals behind the counter. It happened that I walked into a post office, bought stamps and telephone cards, sent a letter by registered mail, and was done within a few minutes. On another occasion, I found the post office staff in the midst of their coffees and cigarettes, seemingly unaware of the people waiting at the counter. Eventually they looked up and started to help people in random order (the discretion line meant nothing to most customers), charging dubious fees in the process.

Telephone

Phoning to Bosnia and Herzegovina: **+387**

Phoning from Bosnia and Herzegovina: **00** – country code – city code without the **0** - number.

Phoning from hotels is often senselessly expensive. Check the prices before you chat away. Phone booths – you will find them at the bus stations and post offices – are a lot cheaper, but still charge more than what you are probably used to. The phones do not accept coins. 10 KM and 20 KM cards can be bought from the post office or at the small newspaper kiosks. Beware: different phone companies provide their services in different parts of the country and your phone cards may not be valid once you leave the town you bought them in.

The companies charge different fees and their nationalist agendas shine through these fees. From Sarajevo, a phone call to Belgrade will cost you quite a bit. Conversely, a call to Belgrade from Banja Luka is considered a local call, and there is no need to even dial the country code. If you intend to make long phone calls, you might even want to cross the entity line if that is only a bus stop away from where you are. In all cases, it is cheaper to phone after 19.00.

Mobile phones have taken Bosnia and Herzegovina by storm. Currently, there are three GSM servers in the country: BiH telecom (061), Eronet (063) and Mobi (065). Unlike the phone card systems, the signals of these servers overlap. This means that, unless you are in the midst of nature or in an isolated village, the signal is generally good.

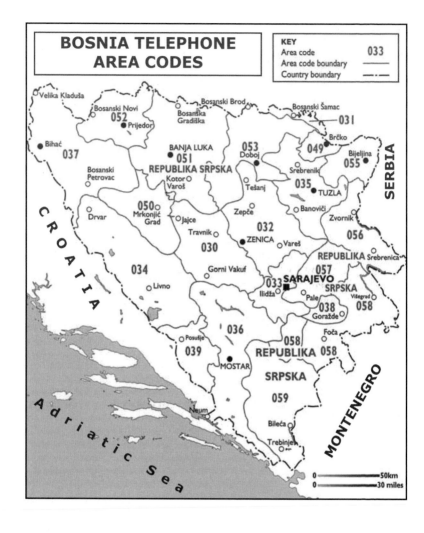

BOSNIA TELEPHONE AREA CODES

KEY
Area code — 033
Area code boundary —
Country boundary —·—·—

European GSM mobiles have roaming agreements with Bosnia and Herzegovina, but roaming prices are high. American and Canadian mobile phones do not allow for roaming at all. In either case, you might want to buy a local SIM card. The first purchase of a local SIM ultra card costs 50 KM, including 10 KM call credit. Call credit is available in the form of 20 KM and 50 KM cards, and can be bought from the post office or at the small newspaper kiosks.

Telephone numbers

Emergencies	124
Police	122
Fire	123
Ambulance	124
Emergency roadside service	1282, 1288
Telegram service	1202
Express delivery (EMS)	1417
Operator, local numbers	1182, 1185, 1186, 1188
Operator, international numbers	1201

Internet

Bosnia and Herzegovina does not have the quick, fluid internet communication that is now common in the West, and has just started to scratch the surface of cyber culture. An increasing number of businesses, including hotels and tourist attractions, have websites and email addresses, but the information content is often limited and emails are not always replied to. Since 2001, internet cafes have been popping up. They typically charge 1 KM per hour and the connections are usually slow. In the main towns, many hotels offer internet connections as well, at various fees.

MONEY

Originally, the KM was pegged to the German mark. With the introduction of the Euro, the KM changed its peg without the least bit of trouble (1.95 KM for 1 Euro). Most shops will accept payment in Euro bills, using a 1 to 2 ratio. There are many ATM machines in all major towns and cities.

US dollars, British pounds, Yens and other major currencies can be exchanged at the banks and exchange offices that are present in most major towns. They also swap your leftover KMs back into any of these main currencies. Most banks do not have a fixed fee, but take a percentage of the total amount. As this percentage varies, you should do a bit of research before exchanging large amounts of money. Travelers' cheques are unusual, and appear to be taken by the Central Profit Bank in the old town of Sarajevo only.

Although credit cards are increasingly widely accepted in major towns, you should not rely on them. Even in the bigger towns almost nobody accepts American Express.

Make sure you have all the cash you need before leaving the major towns, as it is next to impossible to find a money machine or anybody who accepts credit card payments in smaller towns and villages.

In case of emergency: Raiffeisen Bank handles Western Union money transfers.

Normalizing life in Bosnia and Herzegovina

People sometimes get frustrated because, almost a decade after the end of the war, the standard of living is still far below what it was in pre-war Yugoslavia. But there *is* obvious progress in many fields. Take money. In the early post-war period, different parts of the country used to have different currencies. Today, the 'Convertible Mark' (KM or BAM) is fully trusted, experiences little or no inflation, and is accepted anywhere in the country.

BUDGETING

This country is not quite as cheap as the 10 dollar-a-day destinations in the developing world, but if you are used to Western Europe and North America, you will find Bosnia and Herzegovina surprisingly inexpensive. Food, going out, transport: it all costs very little and the prices get even lower when you leave the urban centres.

Most food in Bosnia and Herzegovina is of high quality and very affordable. A fine three-course meal in a good restaurant will cost some 20 to 30 KM, excluding modestly priced beverages. If you have much less to spend it is possible to have a 3 KM meal with pies and yoghurt or to get affordable food from any of the many supermarkets.

Going out is possible whatever your budget. If you have little, do as many Bosnians do: stroll, drink espressos for 1 KM and eat ice cream for 0.5 KM. If you have a little more, a world of possibilities opens up. Cinemas cost 5 KM and theatre tickets set you back between 5 and 25 KM. Discotheques ask relatively high prices (3 to 5 KM) for their drinks but do not usually charge an entry fee.

Transport between cities is very reasonably priced. Mostar to Sarajevo will cost you between 10 and 18 KM, for example. Within town, buses are always cheap, but taxi prices depend on the town you're in. The general rule appears to be: the smaller the town and the lower the number of taxis, the more expensive they are.

In comparison, accommodation seems a little overpriced. Most hotels will not accommodate you for less than 60 KM per night in a single, or less than 75 in a double. If you are a budget traveler, you should not stay in such hotels. Instead, you should pay anything between 15 and 25 KM per night for a bed in a private house. That cuts back costs significantly. If you then spend most days enjoying the city's lively streets and parks, not its restaurants and organized tours and trips, Bosnia and Herzegovina should not cost you more than 40 KM (20 euro) per day.

For hikers and adventure-seekers, day trips cost between 20 and 75 KM. A weekend trip with food, guide, transport and accommodation will cost around 150-200 KM. Week-long trips in the mountains are 700-1,200 KM, fully inclusive.

ACCOMMODATION
Hotels

The war destroyed many of the country's hotels, and in the post-war years many of the remaining hotels housed displaced people rather than tourists. But many new hotels have been built recently and many old ones have been reconstructed or renovated.

The number of stars won't tell you much. First, the categories in the Federation and the Republika Srpska are not the same, and two three-star hotels can be worlds apart. Second, the rating does not consider either the cleanliness or the hotel's atmosphere. To avoid ending up in an uncomfortable pre-war state-owned hotel, it is always wise to check out the hotel before booking in.

The main cities generally have one or more nice and fairly large hotels. Elsewhere, hotels and motels are smaller and usually family-owned. They tend to be affordable and well-kept, and you might be able to bargain a little. Most places include breakfast in the price. Breakfast might be continental or even English in the larger hotels but you are more likely to be served a thin omelet and cheese and jams with bread. Hotels usually offer half board (polu - pansion, with breakfast and dinner) or full board (pun pansion, with breakfast, lunch and dinner), but the price on the price list usually includes breakfast only. Dining out in Bosnia and Herzegovina costs so little that it may both be cheaper and more enjoyable to try out some of the restaurants in town.

There is a 2KM accommodation tax that is not usually included in the price.

Private rooms/apartments

Private accommodation is not as well-organized as in neighboring Croatia but many travel agencies in towns throughout the country do offer accommodation in apartments and private homes. Hosts are invariably friendly, but do not always speak English. A few German words are usually helpful.

In the countryside, you are unlikely to find a room sign or anything else offering private accommodation. But the locals are extremely friendly and it is not offensive to ask somebody for the possibilities. They will probably refuse money but leaving 10KM for coffee and cigarettes is a welcome gesture. Solo women travelers planning to stay in private accommodation should make sure there are other women around.

Campsites

There are quite a few campsites in Bosnia and Herzegovina. Some are close to town, but most are hard to get to and from if you don't have your own transport. Quite a few have a snack bar and toilets only, and cater mostly to day trippers. The best camping opportunities are hard to find, but can be booked through the rafting operators on the Tara, Neretva and Una rivers. It is possible to camp even if you didn't bring either a tent or mats, as some campsites pitch and equip a few tents in the summer period.

Pitching a tent on your own is possible but could be risky if you are not fully confident that you are in a mine-free area.

Mountain lodges

Unfortunately, many of the mountain lodges were destroyed during the war. But some have survived and some others have been reconstructed in the past few years. They have dormitories and a great location, and sometimes offer food. They do not normally have any single or double rooms.

EATING

From whatever angle you look at it: the people in Bosnia and Herzegovina take eating and drinking very seriously. Meals for guests are elaborate and everything is made from scratch. The number of coffee shops, bars, terraces, snack bars and restaurants around the country is mind-blowing. Picnicking families roast their lambs in their entirety. Workers generally receive a 7 to 10 KM 'hot meal allowance' per working day, meant to cover lunch but in reality often a quarter or more of their total remuneration.

Bosnia and Herzegovina's culinary traditions are very strong, and people do not like change. If what you are looking for is not within the tradition of the region, you will have difficulty finding it. The only places that might serve a typical English breakfast are the larger hotels. Pizza has been embraced (if occasionally with mayonnaise), but the Chinese, Indian and Mexican restaurants largely depend on foreigners. If you end up cooking for local people – excluding the people working for one of the international organizations – the chances they'll genuinely enjoy your food are slim.

It's best to go local. Bakeries open early and sell hot rolls, croissants, brown bread and apple and cherry strudels. You can take your breakfast to a café and enjoy it with your morning coffee. Most bakeries will make you a sandwich upon request: white bread with thick slices of cheese and bright pink processed meat with a lot of mayonnaise, generally. A little heavy for breakfast but a must-try for lunch are the famous dishes of burek, zeljanica, sirnica and krompiruša. As everything else, these filo-dough wrapped pies are made from scratch and have been a traditional meal since Ottoman times. Burek is a meat pie. Zeljanica is made from spinach and cheese. Sirnica is made from a fresh, home-made cheese and krompiruša is filo-dough with diced potatoes and spices. They may ask if you like pavlaka spread on top. Pavlaka is a fresh cream that tastes wonderful with the pita. Alternatively, try yoghurt alongside your pita. If you are into local cuisine, ask if you can watch them making these pies: it's amazing how they stretch that dough!

Dinner has more options than breakfast or lunch. The following lists include the most common dishes. Be forewarned that most people in Bosnia and Herzegovina smoke and that non-smoking restaurants do not exist.

Meats

People like eating meat

Soon after my first arrival in Bosnia and Herzegovina, I organized a workshop in a large mountain hut near Zenica. The prices were modest, the rooms looked good, and the food, the man assured me, was excellent. I ordered lunch and dinner for 25

> people. At 13.00, we got five types of meat and fries. At 19.00, we got six types of meat, fries and a small salad. When I expressed my surprise, my colleagues all assured me that these meals were exactly as meals should be.

If you like meat, you will like Bosnia and Herzegovina. Meat is a standard for any meal. With the exception of chicken, most meat is fresh from the mountainside. It is common practice here to raise all animals free range, with plenty of space and without any hormones or chemicals. You will taste the difference.

Bamija	- okra with veal.
Begova čorba	- the most popular soup, made of veal and vegetables.
Bosanski lonac	- meat stew cooked over an open fire.
Ćevapi	- small meat sausages of lamb and beef mix. They are usually served with fresh onions and pita bread on the side.
Filovane paprike	- fried peppers stuffed with minced meat and spices.
Ispod saća	- similar to a Dutch oven. A metal dish is placed on hot coals, the food is placed in the dish and covered by a lid which is then completely covered in hot coals and left to bake.
Janjetina	- lamb grilled over an open fire.
Musaka	- a meat pie made of minced beef, very similar to shepherd's pie.
Pršut	- air-dried ham, similar to Italian prosciutto.
Sarme	- meat and rice rolled in cabbage or grape leaves.
Sogandolma	- fried onions stuffed with minced meat.
Sudžuk	- beef sausages similar to pepperoni.
Suho meso	- dried beef.
Slanina	- dried bacon-like pork.
Teletina	- veal, usually served in cutlets. Veal in Bosnia and Herzegovina is not produced by locking calves in a cage to ensure softer meat.

Cheeses

Iz mjeha - sheep's milk poured into a specially sewn sheepskin 'bag.' After a time the dry cheese is taken out of the skin container and the result is a strong, dry cheese that resembles parmesan.

Kajmak - the most difficult of all cheeses to translate. It is the top layer skimmed from milk, creamy and extremely tasty. Kajmak and uštipak (doughnut-type roll) is a wonderful appetiser.

Livanjski - similar to the dry yellow cheeses of Dalmatia. It is very tasty and usually more expensive than other types of cheese. It originates from the west Bosnian town of Livno.

Mladi sir - literally means young cheese. There isn't an equivalent to it in English. It has a soft texture and is unsalted. Often it is served with a cream sauce on top. It is very healthy.

Travnički - a white, feta-like cheese from the Travnik district in central Bosnia. It is a bit salty and very popular with 'meza', which is the tradition of slow drinking and eating throughout the course of a whole day.

Vlašićki - similar to travnički cheese. It is a highland cheese from the mountain villages on Vlašić Mountain in central Bosnia.

Sweets

Baklava - cake made with pastry sheets, nuts and sugar syrup.

Hurmašica - date-shaped pastry soaked in a very sweet syrup sauce.

Rahatlokum - Turkish delight, a jelly-like candy covered in powdered sugar and often served with Turkish coffee.

Ružica - similar to baklava but baked with raisins in small roll.

Tufahija - stewed apples stuffed with a walnut filling.

DRINKING

Water

Tourism promotion requires simple images. Bosnia and Herzegovina's first countrywide promotional brochure used the country's ancient tombstones. They are old, unique to the country and quite beautiful. Discussing the importance of national symbols at the Sarajevo University, one of the students said she didn't think the tombstone was a very appealing symbol, as the tombstone is linked with death. She suggested using the opposite - life - for future promotion material. She suggested using the country's abundant natural springs.

The student had a point. Pretty much everywhere around the country, water just comes straight out of the ground or the mountainside. Many local water supply systems are not more than a few pipes connected to one of those springs. Almost every town has one of more public fountains – often to be found in front of the mosque – and the water is invariably excellent. There are roadside fountains as well, built long ago for travelers, and most mountain walks will pass by small springs and streams of sparkling fresh water. In short, you have no worries when drinking the water in Bosnia from the tap or elsewhere. It is probably higher quality water than you have at home!

'Mineralna voda' is bottled throughout the country. Try Ilidžanski dijamant, Sarajevski kiseljak, Tešanjski dijamant or Oaza.

Coffee and tea

When in Rome, do as the Romans do. In Bosnia and Herzegovina, they drink coffee. It is the backbone of social life. During the war, when everything was scarce, coffee was amongst the most sought after commodities.

Immediately after the war ended, coffee was the main symbol of a post-war reconciliation campaign. "Tolerance. Let's have a coffee".

Nowadays, coffee is widely available and affordable. The traditional coffee is '*bosanska kafa*'. It is similar to what the rest of the world calls Turkish coffee, and it is served with oddly-shaped sugar cubes and 'rahatlokum' (Turkish delight). By now, espresso and white coffee are available everywhere in towns and cities. In town, an espresso will cost you 1 KM. The other coffees are more expensive. In villages, you may well get your Bosanska kafa for 0.5 KM.

There is a tea drinking tradition as well. You'll enjoy your tea most if you drink what the locals drink. Don't ask for black tea with milk. People here don't drink it, don't know about it and don't serve it well. Try the herbal teas instead. There are a great many types and they generally have a very nice fragrance. They are often organic and come straight from the forest.

Juices

In most places, lemonade and orange juice are the only fresh squeezed juices available. Bottled juices, however, come in all sorts. The locally produced brands – *Swity* being the largest one - are wonderfully delicious. Historically, Croatia and Slovenia produced and sold the final consumer goods, while Bosnia and Herzegovina had specialized in raw commodities and half fabricates. They didn't sell directly to consumers and, consequently, they don't know *how* to sell. The result in the fruit juice sector is that Slovenian and Croatian brands dominate the market, and that the various local brands are still struggling to get the substantial market shares their products deserve. Enough of the economics though, buy local goods – it's good for the country and it's good for you!

Beer

Local beer is cheap. The first word learned by many foreign visitors is pivo. If you like beer, this word is crucial to your trip. A half-liter bottle costs 1 KM in the shop and only 2 or 3 KM in restaurants and bars. Try *Sarajevsko*, *Nektar* and *Preminger*. *Ožujsko* is a good Croatian beer that is also produced locally. In some parts of the Republika Srpska you can find Nikšičko pivo from Montenegro – it's a great beer and according to many locals one of the best in the region. Other imports are available everywhere. They are reasonably priced, but of course more expensive than local beers without really tasting any better.

Wine

The lack of advanced marketing skills shows in the wine sector as it does in the fruit juice sector. The wine-making tradition of Herzegovina dates back to Roman times, and in terms of price and quality the savory reds and dry whites of Herzegovina easily deserve a share in the world wine market. In reality, Herzegovinan wines are rarely seen outside the region. While you're in the country, try them. Stankela, Gangaš žilavka and a range of other sorts will cost you 5 to 20 KM in the shop and 15-35 KM in restaurants.

Spirits

Made from plums, pears, apples or grapes, the local spirits are amazing. They are strong, very strong, with alcohol levels commonly exceeding 40 percent. They are drunk at all times of the day and at all times of the year. Šljivovica (plum) or kruška (pear) are found more in Bosnia. Loza, made of grapes, is the specialty of Herzegovina and Dalmatia (which share the same climate and topsoil and therefore produce very similar grapes). There are a few brand names that you will find everywhere, but the best spirits are home-made. The careful process of making spirits is a male-dominated skill. The Croats in Herzegovina make the best wine and loza, the Serbs make the best šljivovica and kruška. The men who are into producing it will offer a taste of their products as if it were coffee – but with a lot more pride.

PUBLIC HOLIDAYS

Changing every year	Bajrams (Muslim Holy Days)
January 1	New Year
January 7	Orthodox Christmas
January 14	Orthodox New Year
March 1	Independence day
May 1	Labor Day
November 25	Day of the State
December 25	Catholic Christmas

SHOPPING

If you are in any of the main towns, there is a good chance you are close to a 24-hour bakery that took its fresh bread out of the oven just now. The closest grocery shop is probably less than a few minutes away. It is open from the early morning to the late evening, and quite possibly all through the night as well. It sells the exact same products as a thousand other grocery shops around the city. If you need products they do not have, you will succeed in one of the hypermarkets. Snack stands and newspaper kiosks are just around the corner, down town is for fashion and souvenirs, and everything else is spread around the city. There really isn't a thing you can't buy here, and items that are covered separately in guide books to many developing countries (film, sanitary napkins, sun lotion) are all widely available.

Prices in Bosnia and Herzegovina are fixed. While you might successfully try to reduce the price for a room in a family-owned hotel, you would look silly negotiating in Mercator or at the hair dresser. Souvenirs are the exception. When buying souvenirs, you need to bargain a little. Gently though: with rare exceptions, people are not inclined to rip you off at all. Similarly, somebody offering you coffee is not somebody trying to pull off a sales trick: it's what people *do* here.

Certainly unique to the country and the period are the war-related souvenirs. Mortars and bullets are carved and turned into anything from umbrella and candle holders to key chains and pens. Although very contemporary, these war souvenirs are carved in the same Ottoman tradition as the plates and tea and coffee sets. Made of gold, silver, copper, and bronze, all these metal works are good value for money. And they are not merely souvenirs for tourist consumption: unless you buy a plate saying 'best wishes from Bosnia and Herzegovina', you buy something that many Bosnians have at display in their homes. Similarly, the oriental-style rugs and all sorts of woodworks are no pseudo-historical tourist traps, but things that survived the centuries and are still part and parcel of Bosnian life.

INTERACTING WITH LOCAL PEOPLE

Even though there hasn't been a tourist boom since the end of the conflict, the locals are more than familiar with guests from every country in Europe and North America. Ever since the war began in 1992, tens of thousands of people came here as aid workers, soldiers, curious visitors, peace activists, diplomats, businessmen and pilgrims paying homage to the Virgin Mary in Međugorje. Consequently, you will be no surprise to the locals. The locals in the rural areas may stare a bit at first but that seems the thing to do in any small town or village in any other country that I've visited as well. You'll hardly be noticed in places like Sarajevo, Mostar or Banja Luka, where there is a significant international presence.

Local people will almost always be very friendly. This is common to the region but Bosnian hospitality is something special. Bosnians will go out of their way to assist you in finding something and often invite someone to their home for a coffee. Once you enter someone's home as a guest, expect the red carpet treatment. Rich or poor, your host will most certainly serve you coffee, followed by an offer of cigarettes. The unwritten rule is never to light up without offering the people around you a cigarette as well. More than likely the host will bring out sweets (biscuits or chocolate) and if the energy is right out comes the local spirits and food. Coming from the west, one might see it as going a bit overboard, but the tradition of treating guests like one of their own is taken seriously. My advice is to sit back and enjoy, and if you're in a rush – too bad. The best way to turn down the ninth or tenth coffee, or a chunk of meat for the vegetarian (many villagers don't understand the concept) is to say 'ne mogu', which means 'I can't.' Saying 'no, thank you' simply does not work. If you find yourself shaking from the strong Turkish coffees and just want the host to stop filling your cup then leave a bit of coffee in it. As soon as you finish the host will first give you a refill and then ask if you would like some more.

Most young people will speak at least a little bit of English, as it is taught in all the schools from an early age. American movies are popular here and many people have learned English from watching films. In western Herzegovina and northern Bosnia many people speak German. Over 300,000 refugees lived in Germany during the war and many more lived and worked in Germany before the conflict began.

For the most part, young people here don't want to speak about the war or politics. They would rather hear about new music, cool movies, good books or just shoot the breeze with you. The older generation often brings the war and politics into conversation. Many find it therapeutic so lending an ear may be the best service you can offer someone. Comments aren't even necessary. Everyone here bears a burden from the war and oftentimes they cannot handle dealing with someone else's despair. Being a good listener can have a greater effect than one can imagine.

It's nice to exchange addresses, emails, and phone numbers with people. A postcard or phone call when you get home is always much appreciated.

A few rules

People in Bosnia and Herzegovina are very tolerant. It is not easy to offend them, and the warnings that do apply are all in line with common sense.

- People have different ways of dealing with the war. Many prefer not to talk about it. Respect that.

- Begging is one of the very worst forms of child labour. If you give in to it, you encourage it. If you do not give in to it, these poor children may have to continue begging until late at night to ensure a meal or to avoid a beating. It's a dilemma. You might want to consider giving something edible (but no sweets, as these children's nutritional status is generally awful, with a deficit in everything except for sugar).

- In summer especially, the forests get very dry and there are lots of forest fires. Be very cautious.

- Dress whichever way you like, but make sure you are covered when entering a place of worship. Mosques generally have headscarves available at the entrance.

- Ask before you take photographs – refusals are rare. If you promise to send somebody a copy, send that person that copy.

- People are likely to treat you as a guest. Consequently, they would be inclined to pay for you. Remember that most people you will meet have less money than you have. If you want to pay, act quickly and be persistent, or you will fail.

- Tips are optional. Remember that people in the catering business do not normally earn a lot. On the other hand, tips are not really all that common.

Superstitions

Some Bosnians might tell you that they're not superstitious. Well, don't believe them. What some may call superstition many Bosnians take as a natural fact. Where these beliefs have come from nobody knows in full, but rest assured the pagan Illyrians, heretic Bosnian Church, mystic rituals of eastern orthodoxy and Islam have all contributed to them. Here are just a few of the long list of superstitions....

- This one can be refuted (at least by the Bosnians) as a medical fact instead of a superstition. Drafts. Yes, drafts. All diseases are carried in drafts so if its 40 degrees outside and you see all the windows rolled up it's not because everyone has AC. Any earaches, colds, sties, headaches – well, just about any ailment is blamed on that little nip of wind from open windows. Don't be surprised to see people dashing to close the window if there is another one open in the building or car that you're in.

- Drinking anything cold is another great excuse, even in the middle of summer, for why someone is sick. Don't be disappointed, especially American travelers, to find no ice in most places. You'll get sick for heavens sake!

- Wet hair. On more than one occasion during the war one could find Sarajevans taking a brisk walk through sniper fire and shelling – that was normal. God forbid, though, if you stepped outside with wet hair. That is a big no-no. Wet hair, with the combination of wind (yes, even in the summer) will give you pneumonia, guaranteed. If the receptionist looks at you as if you've just been released from a 'home' she or he is simply worried about you. The general rule is you must first dry your hair with a hairdryer, wait at least an hour and then its safe to walk the streets. And you think I'm kidding.

- If you knock a glass over or spill something while speaking – that, of course, means its true.

- When describing an injury or sickness never ever show or explain it on your own body. Never.

- If you spill your coffee, don't fret it, it simply means you are about to be rewarded some material gain.

- An itchy left palm means you are about to get something (positive).

- An itchy right palm, naturally, means you are about to give something.

- An itchy nose means you are about to get angry.

- If you say something you would like to come true be sure to knock on wood three times, but from underneath – the underneath thing is key.

- Whenever entering a building always enter with right foot first.

- Whatever you do don't whistle in the house. It is a sure bet that you have summoned demons and when you leave there is no guarantee that they haven't.

- Bread is heaven's gift. Never throw it away. This rule gained strength in the war due to the extreme lack of food, every crumble was held in high regard.

- Always stir clockwise, it's the natural flow of things.

- It's bad luck to cut your nails after dark. Only daylight cutting please, you don't want to jinx yourself.

- Never stand in the middle of a doorframe...nobody knows why, it's just 'bad.'

- People talking about you makes you hick-up.

That's what we think you need to know to start your journey. Enjoy your trip through the next section!

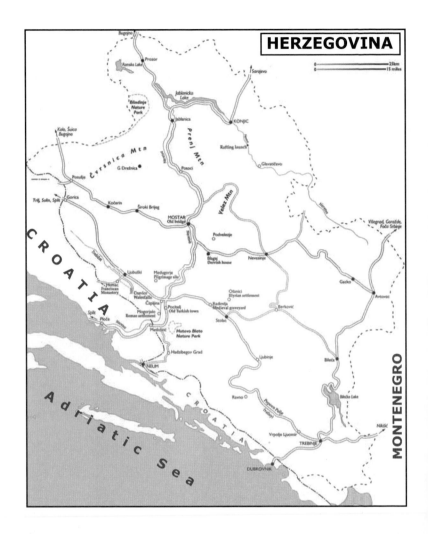

Part two: HERZEGOVINA

Although there are many similarities in language, ethnicity, culture and identity, Herzegovina's history is quite distinct from Bosnia's. In pre-Yugoslavian times, Herzegovina was poorer than Bosnia and Croatia, particularly in rural areas. Surviving was no easy task. Consequently, Herzegovinians came to be hard workers, both on the land and in business, with traditions, rituals and mentalities that are profoundly influenced by the rough geography of the region they live in.

The region was once known as Hum and until the Ottoman conquers in the late 15th century it was ruled by the Kosača family under Herceg Stjepan (or Duke Stjepan) after whom Herzegovina was later named. The history of Herzegovina is a long and fascinating one. In it, all three peoples - Croats, Serbs and Bosniacs - have been present for centuries. Mono-ethnic theories simply have no historical integrity.

The geographical region of Herzegovina is split between the country's two entities – the Federation of Bosnia and Herzegovina in the centre and west, and the Republika Srpska in the east. As everywhere else in the country, there is free movement throughout the region. The western part of Herzegovina is largely Croatian-Catholic and has been so since medieval times. The far eastern part, falling under the Republika Srpska, has become predominantly Serbian-Orthodox after much of its Bosniac-Muslim population fled or was displaced. The central part has a majority Bosniac-Muslim population. These demographic regions broadly correspond with medieval Herzegovina. Centuries of growth had brought the different groups together, but the war drove the groups apart and many people were forced to flee their towns and villages. In the post-war years, there has been a sizeable return flow of Bosniac refugees to Croatian controlled territory. The Serbs, who had a considerable population on the east side of the Neretva valley, have only returned in very small numbers. There is even less – and in some areas a complete absence of - return to Republika Srpska.

Perhaps the starkest contrast you'll find as a traveler in Herzegovina is how relatively 'advanced' the western and central parts of the region are and how generally underdeveloped the far eastern part of the region is. Republika Srpska's part of Herzegovina has been isolated for some time from its traditional center Mostar and economic conditions are very poor. That isolation can be seen in the people too, and some will look at you with a suspicious eye. These conditions have recently begun to change though and you will more than likely have a very pleasant experience with anyone in Herzegovina. My advice is not to talk too much about politics and even less about war. There are very, very different – and distorted - versions of what happened in Herzegovina, and discussing the events can be a most alienating experience.

Many Bosnians would characterize Herzegovina as an arid moonscape. Though some areas of Herzegovina are indeed like that, it also possesses some of the greatest freshwater springs, crystal-clear rivers and endemic types of flora and fauna. The areas around **Jablanica**, **Prozor** and **Konjic** have dense green forests and beautiful serene lakes. The **Trebižat River** has created a wonderful green belt along its banks in Western Herzegovina, as has the Bregava River from the southeast.

A warm Mediterranean climate dominates most of Herzegovina, creating a very different bio-system than that of Bosnia's central and northern regions. Figs, pomegranates, grapes, kiwis, rose hip and mandarins all grow in this sunny region. Many of the finest wines in southern Europe are produced in the small vineyards of western and southern Herzegovina.

Herzegovina has been settled for over 12,000 years and each civilization has left a mark on its rich cultural heritage. This cultural heritage, coupled with the impressive natural beauty of Herzegovina, makes it the most diverse and attractive tourist area in Bosnia and Herzegovina. There are some impressive monuments and stretches of nature here, but for many, the real attractions in Herzegovina are merely the simple but beautiful villages dotting the hillsides and the people therein who work this precious land. Regardless of what you do or where you go, Herzegovina will leave a lasting and positive impression.

NERETVA RIVER

It would be impossible to discuss Herzegovina without mentioning the river, a turquoise gem that has created fertile valleys from Glavatičevo to Doljani and upon which most life in the region thrives. Since ancient times the Neretva has permitted the prosperity and growth of human communities and, as such, omitting the Neretva from the account of Herzegovina would be like writing about Egypt without reference to the Nile.

The Neretva River has its beginnings in Zelengora Mountain in the Borač region and like all rivers in Bosnia and Herzegovina the river initially flows towards the north, or, more precisely in this case, the northwest. In this upper section, the river forces its way between the massifs of the Visočica and Bjelašnica mountains in the north and the massifs of the Crvanj and Prenj Mountains in the south. It flows through numerous canyons and a smaller number of fertile valleys.

Unlike the other rivers in the country, the Neretva River does not succeed in forcing its way exclusively north. Passing to the north of the Prenj massif, the river turns south near the mouth of the tributary Rama. It then forces its way through the canyons between the Prenj and Čvrsnica mountains until it reaches the Mostar Valley where it loses the character of a rapid mountain river. The Neretva then pleasantly meanders through Čapljina into the delta between the Croatian towns of Metković and Ploče, from where it flows into the crystal clear Adriatic Sea.

The Bridge opening ceremony marked a new era for the town of Mostar

Old Bridge spanned the etva River for over 400 years

Fresh produce from all over Herzegovina crowds the summer markets

Reconstruction of the old town was completed in the summer of 2004

Drinking Turkish coffee overlooking ▮ Neretva River is a pastime in Mostar

Dervish order monastery (Tekija) built in the 16th century at the source of the River Buna in Blagaj

Juba diving in the caves at the rce of the Buna River

Fresh juices and Turkish coffee are the in-house specialities at Tekija

Traditional dance festivals occur in Mo
and Blagaj every summer

The Velagić House in Blagaj is one of the
most beautiful examples of
Ottoman architecture

Mostar is situated in a green valley along the Neretva River surrounded by dry
Mediterranean mountain terrain

MOSTAR

A SHORT HISTORY

From Illyrian times until the Ottoman invasion, the ancient settlement of Blagaj was the centre of political power and Mostar was no more than a tiny settlement along the banks of the Neretva. It is believed that before Herzegovina fell to the Ottomans, the settlement of Mostar had only 19 houses with a small suspension bridge that united both banks. The men that guarded this bridge were called mostari (bridge keepers) and it is presumed that the town is named after them.

With the arrival of the Ottomans came relative peace and stability. The mountaintop fortresses, used since Illyrian times and particularly by the Bosnian aristocracy in the centuries before Herzegovina was conquered, lost a great deal of significance. The fertile but exposed valley in which Mostar is located was an ideal place for building a city - so that's exactly what the Ottomans did.

Herzegovina officially came under Ottoman rule in 1482. It didn't take long for Mostar to become the centre of Ottoman administrative and military rule in Herzegovina. The old town (čaršija) that developed around the new stone bridge (Stari most) was completed by Dalmatian craftsmen, but in Ottoman design, in 1566. This oriental part of the city still preserves its old tradition of highly skilled craftsmen in metal engraving, painting and rug-weaving.

With the old bridge at the centre, new mahalas (quarters) began to spring up on both sides of the Neretva. Mosques and medresas (religious schools) were constructed as Islam spread through the growing town. In the late 16th and early 17th centuries, many of Mostar's most beautiful and significant Islamic structures were built. The Čejvan-Čehaj Mosque was constructed in 1552 and is the oldest surviving monument of Ottoman rule in Herzegovina. Arguably the most famous oriental object in Mostar is the Karađoz-beg mosque that was built in 1557. In 1558, eight years before the construction of the Old Bridge, the Kriva ćuprija Bridge was built over the Radobolja Stream that feeds into the Neretva. It was reputedly a prototype for the Old Bridge.

During Ottoman times Mostar quickly became a key trading partner with Dubrovnik and other coastal cities. Caravan routes led directly to Mostar, carrying Dalmatian goods such as olive oil, fish and linen. Cargoes of wool, meat, honey and oats were shipped from Mostar towards the seaside cities. You can still walk the streets of the old town and find craftsmen and artisans of all sorts selling their wares.

In the first two centuries of Ottoman rule, Mostar enjoyed a long peaceful period of cultural, political and economic growth. All three religious communities lived in harmony. Muslims obviously enjoyed more freedoms and tax breaks but the survival and growth of the Christian communities indicates that the Ottomans had a fairly high level of tolerance towards the Christian population. The second half of the Ottomans' four centuries of rule was less peaceful, and strifes and rebellions became commonplace.

After the third failure of the Ottomans in the battle for Vienna in 1683, the empire began its decline. Uprisings were more frequent in the 18th century and in order to appease many of the internal opposing forces, both Muslim and Christian, the Ottomans granted certain freedoms. The old Orthodox Church was renovated in 1833 and a Catholic Church was constructed in 1864.

The end of the 19th century marked the final decline of the Ottomans, and after a three-year uprising throughout the country from 1875 to 1878, the empire collapsed. Opportunistic Austro-Hungary jumped right in and included Bosnia and Herzegovina in its administrative region. A railroad was constructed immediately, adding a European flavor to the oriental town. During the short reign of the Austro-Hungarians, a public bath was built, many newspapers and periodicals were established, more schools and bridges were erected and the city expanded its road system. All along the outskirts of the old town one can see the Viennese-style architecture from this period.

Austro-Hungarian rule ended with the assassination of Prince Ferdinand in Sarajevo. In the decades that followed, much of Bosnia and Herzegovina experienced harsh economic and political struggles. With the end of World War II and the victory of Tito's partisans came a challenging but, especially after the late 1950s when Tito had consolidated his power, peaceful time. Mostar became one of the major socialist strongholds in the former Yugoslavia. It had the highest rate of mixed marriages and continued to be the most important city of Herzegovina. The city enjoyed great prosperity in the years leading up to the disintegration of Yugoslavia. That all changed when the Yugoslav National Army (JNA), backed by paramilitary groups from Serbia and Montenegro, stormed Mostar. This was followed by a split in the Muslim-Croat forces, when the Croatian army turned on their former allies. In the recent war Mostar experienced more destruction than in any other war in its history and amongst the worst destruction of any urban area in Bosnia and Herzegovina.

PRESENT-DAY

Until 2004, Mostar was split up along ethnic lines and consisted of six small municipalities. To the visitor the ethnic division may not be evident, but nationalist parties on both sides had redrawn Mostar's municipal boundaries to suit their demographic dominance. Some Croats see Mostar as the capital of their self-declared state, and the ruling nationalist parties support its partition. The Bosniacs view Mostar more as a united town, but the Bosniac nationalist parties still try to maintain their demographic stronghold on the predominantly Muslim east bank. These corrupt and outdated policies are robbing the local residents of a normal, stable life and hopes of a better future. A recent decision of the country's High Representative to unify the six municipalities into the "City of Mostar", guaranteeing equal rights and representation to all its peoples, has been most courageous. This vision of a truly united Mostar is the only way to ensure that future generations will enjoy peace.

There has been much reconstruction since the war ended but scenes of almost complete destruction can still be seen along the former confrontation line on the main boulevard. Many true Mostarians are now refugees in Europe and America, unwilling to return to a divided city. The wounds will take a long time to heal.

THE OPENING OF THE NEW BRIDGE

When the Stari most, or Old Bridge, collapsed from tank shelling in 1993 it was like the heart was ripped out of most Mostar natives. Even mentioning the bridge for years after it fell to the bottom of the Neretva River could invoke tears as it symbolized both the city and the country as a whole. Now, more than a decade later, the beautiful stone structure that had spanned the Neretva River for over four centuries once again arches across its raging waters. The bridge opening in July 2004 was spectacular – with almost every major television station around the world covering the event.

The music, the fireworks, the traditional diving from the crest of the 21 meter high bridge were witnessed by tens of thousands of people from around the country and by tourists and dignitaries from around the world. Although it was portrayed as a symbol of bridging the Bosniac east and Croat west side of the city, the Stari Most actually does nothing of the sort: both ends are in 'Bosniac-controlled territory'. Most Mostar natives consider that irrelevant – the bridge is Mostar's core and its reconstruction means that life is slowly but surely returning to normal in what is most certainly the most beautiful city in Bosnia and Herzegovina.

GETTING THERE AND AROUND

Mostar Airport (www.mostar-airport.ba).

The airport was 'no man's land' during the conflict and was heavily damaged. It has been renovated but doesn't yet see many planes flying in. The ones that do fly in tend to be charter flights for Catholic pilgrims to Međugorje. Generally, it is much easier to find flights into Split or Dubrovnik in neighboring Croatia, or to fly into the capital Sarajevo.

There is a taxi service to the city centre, which is only 3-4km away. A taxi ride to the centre costs 10-15KM depending on the hotel, the amount of luggage and the honesty of your driver. The bus service from Mostar Airport runs at 06.45, 07.30, 14.00 and 15.30 from Monday to Saturday and at 07.30, 14.00 and 15.30 on Sunday. Most taxi drivers accept euros, and it is best to change your currency to KM once you're in town.

Split Airport

You can get a flight to Split (mostly via Zagreb) from any major city in Europe. From there, it is a three- to four-hour drive to Mostar.

There is a shuttle service from the airport to the bus station, from where buses go to Mostar at least five times per day. You need Kuna, the Croatian currency, to buy your bus ticket. You can get your Kuna at the airport, where the post office usually offers better exchange rates than any of the various airport banks.

Trains

The trains are cheap and comfortable, and the schedule is simple:

Mostar - Ploče	8:56; 21:40
Mostar - Sarajevo	7:10; 17:20

Buses

Local transport is excellent in and around Mostar. **Mostar Bus**, located at the main bus and railway station, covers the town and most of the surrounding areas (Čapljina, Počitelj, Blagaj) with routes that run all day long. Bus fares within the city are usually 1KM for a one-way trip within the city limits, regardless of how far the destination. The Mostar Bus schedules change too frequently to print them here, but the Mostar Bus office in the main bus station is helpful and has current schedules (tel: 036 552 025).

Schedules for longer inter-city lines are only slightly more stable. In October 2004, these schedules were as follows:

Within Bosnia and Herzegovina

Mostar - Konjic	07:45; 12:00; 16:45
Konjic - Mostar	09:00; 14:15; 18:15
Mostar - Nevesinje	11:00
Nevesinje - Mostar	13:45
Mostar - Gacko	08:00
Gacko - Mostar	10:00
Mostar - Bugojno - Zenica	10:20; 16:00
Zenica - Bugojno - Mostar	15:40; 09:20
Mostar - Konjic - Sarajevo	06:00; 07:00; 09:00; 11:00; 15:00; 18:15
Sarajevo - Konjic - Mostar	06:00; 09:00; 11:30; 12:30; 15:30; 18:00; 19:55
Mostar - Zagreb	09:00
Zagreb - Mostar	08:00
Mostar - Split	07:00; 09:45; 10:15; 12:45; 23:30
Split - Mostar	09:30; 16:00; 21:00
Mostar - Korčula	3:30 (Tuesday, Friday, Saturday)
Korčula - Mostar	(Wednesday, Thursday, Sunday)
Mostar - Međugorje	09:00; 10:15; 16:30; 19:10
Mostar - Herceg-Novi	07:00
Mostar-Dubrovnik	07:00 (Glob tour); 10:00 (CTS); 24:45
Dubrovnik - Mostar	08:00; 17:00; 22:30
Mostar - Varaždin - Vukovar	20:20
Mostar - Trebinje	06:15; 12:30; 15:30 (working days only)
Mostar - Grude	19:10
Mostar - Neum	07:00; 10:00
Neum - Mostar	18:30 (Glob tour)
Mostar - Banja Luka	13:30
Mostar - Sarajevo - Tuzla	16:00
Mostar - Sarajevo - Zenica	17:00
Mostar - Tuzla	04:50(Ljajić tours); 06:30 (Salineatrans); 16:00(Salineatrans)

International lines

Mostar - Dortmund	07:00 (Sunday)
Dortmund - Mostar	05:00 (Tuesday)
Mostar - Stockholm	04:00 (Wednesday)
Stockholm - Mostar	07:00 (Saturday)

Taxis

Taxi rates are standard: 3KM to start and 1KM for each additional kilometer. As Mostar is tucked neatly into a valley and fairly compact, a taxi anywhere around town shouldn't cost more than 10KM. Taxi's in Mostar are a bit harder to come by than in other cities in Bosnia and Herzegovina, and we have repeatedly had drivers not turning on their meters and charging double at journey's end. Apologies to all the hard working and honest taxi drivers in Mostar – but getting burned more than once inspired this warning to other travelers.

TOURIST INFORMATION

One of the biggest problems in all of Bosnia and Herzegovina is up-to-date information for visitors. You will find some pamphlets at the hotels and, of course, more information is available at the Tourist Information Centre in the old town (tel: 036 580 833; email: info@touristinfomostar.co.ba; web: www.touristinfomostar.co.ba), but it's all fairly unimpressive. There are plenty of books about Mostar, but still no comprehensive new travel guides. Much of the material you will find contains pre-war material and photos. The best available short guide is 'Mostar and its Surroundings', which you can find in the new Tourist Information Centre on the west bank of the old town and at Fortuna Tours on Kujundžiluk on the east bank. This guide offers a short summary of the history, culture, art and things to see and do. It also has a nice color tourist map showing information centers, banks, post offices, police station, telephones, parking and taxi stands. It lacks, however, practical information on hotels and restaurants and the like.

A Herzegovina website (www.hercegovina.ba) offers quite a bit of information on Mostar. If all goes as planned, a 'Greetings from Mostar' cd-rom with photos, a film and lots of practical information will reach the souvenir shops some time in 2005 (a Studio 7 production, probably retailing at 10KM) .

TOUR OPERATORS

Fortuna Tours Mostar Trg Ivana Krndelja 1; tel: 036 552 197, 061 198 178; fax/tel: 036 551 888; www.fortuna.ba; e-mail: fortuna@cob.net.ba. Fortuna Tours is the largest tour operator working in Mostar. They have offices at the main bus/train station and in the old town by the Stari Most on Kujundžiluk St. They offer accommodation, information and guided tours at prices that depend on the size of the group and the season. They can organise trips in other areas of Bosnia and Herzegovina and Croatia as well.

Astra Travel; Blagaj bb; tel: 036 571 463, 061 106 016; email: astratours_mostar@yahoo.co.uk. They are located in Blagaj and can arrange private accommodation, tours around Blagaj and the Mt. Velež region as well as the greater Herzegovina area.

Almira Travel; Mala Tepa br. 9; tel: 036 551 873, 061 212 570; fax: 036 551 873; email: a.travel@bih.net.ba; www.almira-travel.ba (in German only). Almira Travel offers quite a number of summer excursions throughout Herzegovina, and winter trips to the country's various ski destinations. They offer guided tours through Mostar too, for 100KM for groups from 20 to 50 people (excluding 4KM per person for entry tickets for the Turkish house and a mosque), or 10KM per person if the group is smaller (but not too small, and also excluding the same 4KM for entrance tickets).

Bon Voyage; Rade Bitange 9; tel: 036 580 229, 061 148 980; e-mail: torlos@cob.net.ba. Bon Voyage Tours is situated beautifully in a very green villa, immediately next to one of Mostar's smaller streams. They offer the entire range of tourism services from cold drinks and internet access to accommodation and excursions. Their guided tours through Mostar cost 100 KM per hour for groups up to 30 (you might be able to bargain if your group is small). Bon Voyage sometimes closes its doors in the low season.

Atlas, Kardinala Stepinca bb; tel: 036 326 631; e-mail: atlas-ambasador.medjugorje@tel.net.ba

Comoder; Dr. Ante Starčevića 32; tel: 036 319 201; e-mail: comoder-iata@tel.net.ba; web: www.doom.ba-comoder

Reise Service; Dubrovačka bb; tel: 036 314 888; e-mail: reise-service@tel.net.ba; web: www.reise-service@max.net.ba

Kompas; Kneza Domagoja bb; tel: 036 333 050

Globus; Kralja Tomislava (lamela 1); tel: 036 325 551; e-mail: globusmostar@max.net.ba

WHERE TO STAY

Although Mostar is once again a very popular summer destination, the pre-war visitor numbers have not yet been matched and finding a place to stay is usually not that difficult. International booking is not general practice as of yet, but if you are visiting from Sarajevo or the Dalmatian coast most travel agencies can book you a room before you arrive. As a general rule, most hotels have rooms with private facilities, bar and restaurant, and many accept credit cards. Private pensions usually accept cash only (KM or euros.)

Hotel prices are very reasonable. The only luxury hotel in town charges 160KM or more for a night. The other large hotels start at 53KM and smaller hotels typically charge between 30 and 70KM. In some cases, rates are higher from June to August. Most prices include breakfast but be sure to ask if it's a buffet breakfast or just a piece of toast with jam and a cup of coffee.

Luxury

Bevanda Stara Ilinčka bb; tel: 036 332 332; fax: 036 332 335; email: hotel.bevanda@tel.net.ba; web: www.hotelbevanda.com. Bevanda is rumored to be the best hotel in the country. The service is second to none. The rooms are large with chic art decor. Suites come with a large jacuzzi.

Rooms have AC, phone, satellite TV and a minibar. The building itself is spacious and the restaurant offers a wide range of European dishes and local specialties as well as a wine menu that is not exclusively local. Single/double rooms cost 160/240KM and suites cost 400KM per night. There is a private parking garage below the hotel.

First class

Hotel Bristol Mostarskog bataljona bb; tel: 036 500 100; fax: 036 500 502; email: bristol@cob.net.ba; web: www.bristol.co.ba. The Bristol was destroyed during the war and renovated some years ago. The terrace overlooking the lovely Neretva River is a popular spot for local businessmen and politicians. A single costs 72KM per night and a double 110KM. The rooms have AC, minibar, phone and satellite TV.

Hotel Ero Dr. Ante Starčevića bb; tel: 036 386 777; fax: 036 386 700; email: hotel.ero@tel.net.ba; web: www.ero.ba. When the war ended, the European Union administered the town from Hotel Ero. For the price of 79KM for a single and 136KM for a double you get a comfy room with satellite TV, minibar, telephone and AC. The restaurant serves good food and the reception is very helpful in assisting you with whatever you may need.

Hotel Mostar Kneza Domagoja bb; tel: 036 322 679; fax: 036 315 693; the hotel website (www.hotelmostar.com) appears to be out of order. This is the oldest standing hotel in town. Hotel Mostar offers nice but simple accommodation. The rooms are not air-conditioned and they are stocked with only the basic phone and TV (no satellite). If you're not looking for luxury but would like the convenience of a medium-sized hotel, the single rate of 53KM and double of 86KM is not a bad deal.

Tourist class

Villa Rose Bulevar bb; tel/fax: 036 578 300; email: info@pansion-rose.ba; web: www.pansion-rose.ba. A great, inexpensive place just off the main boulevard in Donja Mahala. For the price of 30KM per person you get a comfy and clean room with bathroom, shower and television. Breakfast is included. The hosts go out of their way to make your stay as comfortable as possible. From Rose, it is a short walk to the old bridge. They also have private parking and internet connection for 1KM per hour.

Pansion Tanović Kriva Ćuprija 2; tel: 061 135 286. A new pension just next to the Pavarotti Centre in the old town. It has two double rooms with bathrooms and a small shared kitchen. The bigger and better room has a balcony. They charge 30KM per person. In quiet times, you can get your own room for 40KM. Longer periods get you a discount: I once paid 500 KM for a month. Mr. Tanović has another beautiful little place on the other side of the river.

Pansion Most Adema Buće 100; tel: 036 552 528; fax: 036 552 660; email: pansion_most@yahoo.com. This private house is conveniently located in Černica, not far from the Old Bridge.

Zdrava hrana Alikalfića 5; tel: 036 551 444. Located in the Brankovac area on the east bank. Bed and breakfast costs 30KM but for groups of more than three they offer a discount. Zdrava hrana doesn't have a restaurant or any common rooms. Breakfast is, in fact, served in your room.

Fortuna Tours Trg Ivana Krndelja 1; tel: 036 551 888; email: fortuna@cob.net.ba; web: www.fortuna.ba. This travel agency, with offices in the main train station and on Kujudžiluk near the Old Bridge, has a great network of private accommodation.

Motel Han Put za Opine bb; tel. 036 577 366; fax: 036 577 777; e-mail: motelhan@mostar.ba, web: www.motel-han.mostar.ba. This hotel is a bit out of town near the suburb of Opine – which is southeast of the center of town. It is a new hotel with nice rooms, but there isn't much of a view and it's not very close to the center of town. It has AC, satellite television, and a restaurant and café on the ground floor.

Pansion Ćorić; Fra Didaka Buntića 125 a; tel. 036 331 077. This small place is centrally located and provides good accommodation at relatively low rates.

WHERE TO EAT

Mostar is no exception to the café culture that dominates Bosnia and Herzegovina. If you're only up for a coffee or a refreshing drink all restaurants will gladly serve you. If you ask for a menu the tempting traditional meals and extremely low prices may convince you to stay a bit longer.

Traditional menus of 'just off the mountainside' meats and cheeses from Herzegovina are always popular with visitors. Dalmatian-style foods, especially sea fish, have long been a local favorite in this inland Mediterranean city. Like most places in Herzegovina you'll also be able to find a good pizza or an Italian dish of some sort. Salads are not the elaborate Western type, but you can bet that the vegetables are home-grown and very tasty. Herzegovina's ancient tradition of winemaking means that high-quality local wines are very affordable. A good bottle of white or red wine shouldn't cost more than 35KM.

It would be impossible to list all the good restaurants in town. Wandering around and choosing a place at your leisure is a safe bet: I've yet to come across a bad restaurant in Mostar.

ABC Fejćeva St. bb; tel: 061 194 656. This has always been known as the best sweet shop in town. They've expanded their horizons though and built a classy but inexpensive restaurant on the first floor. Much of the menu is obviously aimed at foreign guests, offering a good selection of salads (real salads, not just cabbage and tomato), pizzas, European dishes and of course the local favorites.

Stari mlin Jusovina bb; tel: 061 285 041. Stari mlin means old mill and that's exactly what purpose this restaurant served at one point. Now it is a quaint restaurant with a standard traditional menu and intimate ambience.

Babilon Taphana bb; tel: 036 580 574, 061 164 912. This must be named after the Babylon-like walls of the old town. The multi-terraced restaurant has one of the best views of the Old Bridge and the powerful Neretva racing below it. The grapevines draped above keep it cool even on the hottest days. The food is good and the servings are large. Meals range from 5KM to 15KM.

Hindin han Jusovina 10; tel: 061 153 924. With 8-15KM entrees you can't go wrong in this authentic traditional restaurant. Han specializes in locally made cheeses, meats and wines. The wine menu runs from 10KM to

30KM per bottle of exclusively domestic products. The kitchen is open late.

M&M nacionalni restoran Bataljona bb; tel: 036 580 192. For when you're in a hurry: excellent traditional food in fast-food format. The food is ready and at display. You choose what you want and get it right away.

Taurus Kriva ćuprija 1; tel: 061 212 617. This traditional restaurant near the Kriva ćuprija serves local, Italian and Dalmatian dishes. They're also big on fish, offering calamari, shark, trout and eel, to name just a few. The rustic decor and fireplace make it a great place for dinner and the small terrace on the Radobolje is a great spot for lunch.

Restoran Kraljice Katarine 11a; tel: 036 561 100. Finding this place may be your greatest Radobolja challenge but when you do you won't be disappointed. Situated at the source of the Radobolja River, it's a wonderfully refreshing spot for trout, Dalmatian specialties and good quality pršut or ham.

Šadrvan Jusovina 11; tel: 036 579 057; email: bjanka_krpo@hotmail.com. The name means 'fountain' in the local language. It appropriately has an Ottoman-style fountain in its front garden. This restaurant serves the standard traditional and Dalmatian dishes, with a similar wine menu as the others. Šadrvan serves vegetarian food too and most dishes are only 5KM. You may find seasonal live music as well.

Other restaurants to visit around Mostar

Aster, 036 341 161, Cim smrčenjaci 14 b

Fontana kod soče, 036 311 182, Rudarska 174

Hercegovina, 036 324 469, Zagrebačka bb

Hladovina, 036 311 118, K. Branimira 4

Konoba, 036 381 167, Goranci-centar bb

Kubat, 036 341 550, Goranačka 1

Dallas, 036 550 065, Trg Ivana Krndelja 6

WHAT TO SEE

The old Ottoman town has always been the main attraction in Mostar. It is very compact and ideal for walking. Most of the main tourist sights can be seen in a one-day tour. There are almost as many café's in Mostar as there are pubs in London, so it's never difficult to find a cool spot to take a break from the hot Herzegovina sun. The old town has an enticing quality, particularly on the Neretva, which often leads one to sit for hours and just soak up the sights and sounds. Unlike most tourist places in the world, café and restaurant owners will never ask you to leave even if you've been sipping a Turkish coffee for hours. The old town has been reconstructed almost in its entirety. In it, there are countless shops of coppersmiths and artists at work as well as several fascinating antique shops.

A walking tour through Mostar

The Tourist Information Centre on the west bank of the old town and most tour operators on both sides of the river are able to arrange guided tours around Mostar in most European languages. Alternatively, you could make the walk we suggest here:

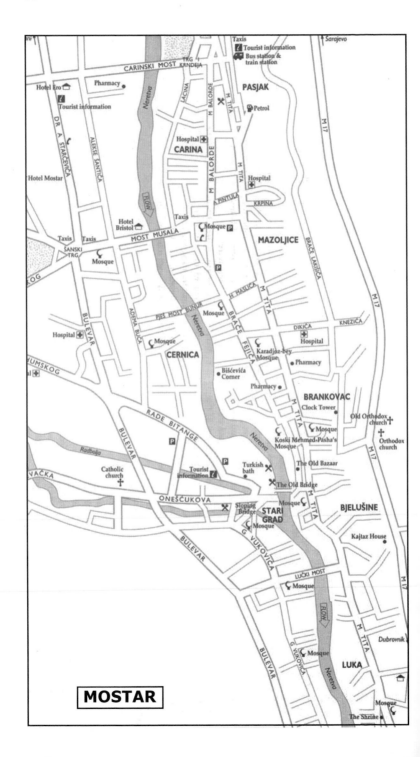

MOSTAR

Starting from the bus station at the north end of town head west across the **Carina Bridge**. Just before Hotel Ero on the left is **Šantića Street**. Aleksa Šantić was a famous poet who fell in love with a Muslim woman named Emina. Being a Christian he was not permitted to marry her and although he was willing to convert to Islam to win her love her family would not allow it. One of the most famous sevdalinkas (traditional love songs) was written in her honor.

This street was the dividing line between the Croatian and Bosnian forces and saw some of the most intensive fighting of the whole war. In between colorful reconstructed buildings, you can still see what this place looked like in 1994. Taking the second street to the right (the one with the beautiful old mosque at the corner), the road rises to meet the Bulevar (Boulevard). You soon reach the **Spanish Square** with its life-size open-air chess board and a monument that commemorates the Spanish soldiers that died here in 1993 and beyond. Next to it, there is the **Old Gymnasium**. Though Moorish in appearance, this gymnasium was completed in 1898 during the Austro-Hungarian occupation of the country. From the outside, the building still looks battered, but some of the classrooms have been restored and refurbished, and were taken into use in the summer of 2004.

Turning left onto Bulevar and continuing south is a walk down the very line that still effectively divides Mostar's eastern and western sides. The remaining scenes of destruction flanking this street are sobering reminders of the war. Turn left at the next traffic lights, and right again when you reach the parking lot in front of the modern building that currently houses the High Representative's office in Mostar. Take a left at the other side of the parking lot, and you'll quickly reach the entrance to the old Ottoman town. Here, the street turns into an old cobblestone footpath.

From here, quaint souvenir shops and galleries line the narrow streets of the Old Town as you near the Old Bridge. On the right, there is the oldest single arch stone bridge in Mostar, the **Kriva ćuprija** (Sloping Bridge), built in 1558 by the Ottoman architect Čejvan Kethoda. On the left, you'll find the best book shop in town. Buybook has a great selection of local and international literature available in English.

Just before you reach the Old Bridge you will see a small alleyway to the left, leading to a complex that used to be the **Hamam and Tabhana Turkish Baths.** The complex was heavily damaged during the war but all was restored and the courtyard and terrace are now a favorite gathering place for the young and old, sitting to enjoy a coffee or a meal on the terraced walls that offer one of the best views of the Old Bridge. The Turkish baths, recognizable by the six domes, were built in the 16th century and now function as a cultural centre and art gallery.

No matter how many times one does it, crossing the **Stari most** (Old Bridge) always seems to be an exciting experience. This single-arch stone bridge is an exact replica of the original bridge that stood for over 400 years and that was designed by Hajrudin, a student of the great Ottoman architect Sinan. It spans 28.7 meters of the Neretva river, 21 meters above the summer water level. Don't let the irritating show-divers, sometimes almost aggressively demanding money from passers-by, spoil the experience!

The **Halebija and Tara towers** have always housed the guardians of the bridge and during Ottoman times were storehouses for ammunition.

Crossing from the west bank to the east you'll also be crossing the ancient point where East and West symbolically met. Up the stairs to the right is the oldest mosque in Mostar: the **Čejvan Čehaj Mosque** built in 1552. Later a medresa (Islamic school) was built on the same compound.

Turn left down the stairs and you will find the Old Bazaar, **Kujundžiluk.** Named after the goldsmiths who traditionally created and sold their wares on this street, it is the best place in town to find authentic paintings and copper or bronze carvings of the Stari Most, pomegranates (the natural symbol of Herzegovina) or the famed stećaks (medieval tombstones). On the occasion of the opening of the reconstructed Stari Most, this entire area was renovated in the summer of 2004, and now looks absolutely splendid once again.

Carpet-makers, coppersmiths and antique collectors all continue to pass on the tradition of stari zanati (old crafts) from father to son. Kujundžiluk heads slightly up hill and here is the best photo opportunity to catch the awesome grace and beauty of the Stari most. At the top of the hill the old town continues to the left and is lined with yet more shops. Here you'll find carpet-makers and boutiques that sell the traditional attire of Herzegovina. These shops are rare and if you're a collector or just interested in the oldstyle wares of Herzegovina your best bet is probably here.

To the left through a small archway is the **Koski Mehmed paša Mosque**, built in 1617. It is open to visitors and free of charge. Feel free to walk down to the šadrvan (fountain) and have a cool drink of water. Visitors may enter the mosque and take photos free of charge. Although it isn't always required, it is customary to remove shoes before entering. Women are not required to cover themselves as this mosque was especially designated to show Mostar's many guests the beauty of Ottoman Islamic architecture. The paintings inside are typical of Ottoman design and the detailed woodwork of the doors is an Ottoman trademark. The altar with steps is for the efendija (Muslim cleric) to lead prayers or to address his congregation. For those willing to bear the dizzy spiral to the top, the minaret is also open to the public and is accessible from inside the mosque. The view speaks for itself!

Carrying on to the left after leaving the mosque you will find the **Tepa Market**. This has been a busy marketplace since Ottoman times. It now sells mostly fresh produce grown in Herzegovina. When in season, the figs and pomegranates can't be beaten. Be sure to look for local honey, organically produced in sunny villages all over Herzegovina. A large jar costs around 10KM.

Heading north now, on **Fejića Street** is the nightclub and café district. It's quite small and certainly lively in the evenings. For those looking for a little more tranquility than the clubs and café's can offer, the **Bišćevića House** is a little further up to the left on **Bišćevića Street.** This 17th-century Ottoman house rests (some parts on pillars of over 5m long) on the eastern banks of the Neretva. There is a conversation or gathering room or divanhan preserved in authentic Ottoman style. Throughout the house are original household objects and the courtyard is a fine example of the Ottoman style. The entrance fee to the house is only 3KM.

Back on Fejića Street, a short distance to the north is the Karađozbegova Mosque. This is the most important and significant of sacred Islamic architecture in all of Herzegovina. Completed in 1557, its designer was Kodža Mimar Sinan, a great Ottoman architect. The interior, typically Ottoman in style, has lost much of its detailed paintings through water damage. This mosque was also heavily bombarded during the war and its minaret was completely destroyed by tank and artillery rounds from the Croatian forces. Reconstruction is in progress, and you can already enter (2KM) and climb the minaret (an additional 3KM).

Continuing your stroll down Fejića you will see more café's and the **ABC sweet shop** and restaurant. This is a favorite local hangout for good ice-cream and is a great place to sit and people-watch.

Follow the street for a few more minutes (this includes a turn left and a turn right) and you'll end up at one of the main squares in town. Tito built his villa right next to the famous **Hotel Neretva** here. Sadly, both these buildings were destroyed in the war. Their ruins stand in stark contrast with the reconstructed **public baths,** also lining the square. This building, like the Old Gymnasium a short way across the river, was built in pseudo-Moorish style during Austro-Hungarian times. The public baths' beautiful swimming pool is open for a swim (2KM; tel: 036 397 350).

If you cross the river and pass Hotel Bristol, you'll find the Šantića Street you walked on at the beginning of this walk on the right hand side. That concludes the neat circle tour of the old town.

Other places to see

A city map would help you to find Mostar's other interesting places. Most of them can easily be reached by foot.

The **Museum of Herzegovina** (Bajatova 4; tel/fax: 036 551 602) is situated in a beautiful part of the Old Town. It was founded in 1950 to promote the archaeological, ethnographic, literary and cultural history of Herzegovina. The museum is open from 09.00 to 14.00 on weekdays and from 10.00 to 12.00 on Saturday and costs 1.50 KM. It was closed for renovations when I last checked, but should be open again by the time of publishing.

A bit off the centre circuit of the old town is the best-preserved Otto-man-style house in Herzegovina called the **Kajtaz House** (Gase Ilića 21; tel: 036 550 913). The Kajtaz House has been named a UNESCO heritage site and is now protected by law as the finest example of an Ottoman home. Fortuna Tours near the Old Bridge can arrange a tour guide or you can wander up to the house yourself. The host does not speak English but she will gladly walk you through the oldstyle kitchen with all its original and functional furniture and equipment. The garden terrace, shadowed by Hum Mountain to the west, has plenty of seats. Sit back and enjoy the hostess's home-made juice made from rose petals - it is absolutely amazing and nearly impossible to find anywhere else. The upstairs floor is laid out in typical Ottoman fashion. There are separate sleeping rooms for the women, all with bathing areas within the room. The women also had a large sitting room where they would receive guests and entertain. The men lived in the southern part of the house but the man of the house had free range to visit his wives. The wooden wardrobes and large chests are carved with intricate oriental designs. In the open foyer upstairs you can try on a set of tradi-tional attire (men and women's) - a great photo opportunity. The fact that the house is still lived in adds to its charm.

The British charity **War Child** was very active in Mostar during and after the war. They managed to gather many famous singers, including

Bono and Pavarotti. Together, they raised sufficient funds to build a music centre. The **Pavarotti Music Centre** on Titova Street in the Brankovac area gives the people of Mostar, particularly the younger generation, an opportunity to learn, create and play music with modern equipment and facilities. There is a café in the main lobby that exhibits local art. Foreigners often visit to drink a coffee and have a chat with local musicians and artists. It is open to the public seven days a week. Sadly, the center's management doesn't make the most out of this great place, and very often it's completely empty.

One of most beautiful religious structures in Mostar was the **New Orthodox Church.** The war unfortunately erased this fine example of Byzantine architecture. Remains of the older **Orthodox Church**, located on the same grounds, is still an interesting place to visit, as is the old cemetery next to it. The folktale behind the construction of the New Orthodox Church is included below.

The old **Catholic Church**, which was recently renovated, is nearly impossible to miss. A steeple of over 30m dominates the skyline. The church was heavily damaged during the war and reconstruction has been completed only recently.

The **bishop's residence** in Mostar marks the long Catholic traditions of the region and is built in the Viennese architecture that greatly added to the town's charm. The roundabout by the **Rondo** on the west side is home to the former Cultural Centre for the City of Mostar. It is now the **Croatian Cultural Centre** and certainly worth a peek inside. The somewhat bulky and markedly socialist **Partisan Memorial Cemetery** commemorates the fallen Communists. It is located off KP Krešimira IV Street on Bijeli Brijeg. This part of town is covered with lots of greenery and is also a nice place for a stroll with a great view of the city.

You may notice that on top of the hill (hum) in the centre of town a large cross has been erected. Although this is common in the Italian countryside it is a fairly new practice in Herzegovina. The cross above Mostar, however, is seen by many as a very provocative landmark. During the war, from the exact spot where the cross is erected, the Croatian forces pummeled east Mostar with artillery and anti-aircraft fire. Due to the no-fly zone enforced by NATO during the war there were no planes to fire at so the anti-aircraft weapons were fired at civilians. It is a painful reminder to many citizens not only of the brutal war that divided the city but also of the deep rifts in relations between the ethnic groups today.

The myth of the New Orthodox Church

The Serbian priest had gone to the beg (local ruler in Ottoman times) to ask permission to build a new church. It was often the custom, especially for non-Muslims, to offer the beg some sort of gift. The beg already had something in mind and asked for the priest's daughter. When the priest refused, his request for the church was rejected and he was sent away. The priest, however, would not give up. He returned, insisting that he be allowed to build a church. The old church was no longer big enough to suit the growing Orthodox community and it was imperative that he be granted permission for both the land and the church. The beg again questioned the priest about his lovely daughter, but the

Međugorje has become the second largest Catholic pilgrimage site in the world

...ite of the vision of the Virgin Mary ...s worshippers from all over the world

Apparition Hill, Međugorje's holy mountain

The Arslanagić Bridge in Trebinje

Herzegovina has a long tradition of fine red wines

Humac Monastery near Ljubuški hos oldest museum in Bosnia and Herze

Neum, Herzegovina's tourist destination on the Adriatic Sea

he sunny Mediterranean climate produces a rich array of fruits including lemons, limes, figs, pomegranates and kiwi's

Kravice Waterfalls on the Trebižat River near Ljubuški

Počitelj near Čapljina is perhaps the finest example of a quaint Ottoman town

Mogorjelo near Čapljina was th of an ancient Roman settlemen

priest would hear nothing of it. Again he was sent away without the blessing of the beg. After returning yet once more the annoyed beg conceded - but under one condition. The land to be given by the authorities would be no larger than the woolen jumper worn by the priest. The priest left, discouraged and angry, but as he walked home a brilliant idea struck him. He was a large man and the jumper consisted of dozens of meters of wool when it was unpicked and all laid out. The priest brought this jumble of yarn to the beg and calculated that if he spread the entire contents of the yarn from his jumper it would be large enough to build a new church. The beg was so tickled by the priest's ingenious mind that, with a chuckle, he granted the hardheaded priest permission to build the church.

AROUND MOSTAR

Herzegovina is a relatively compact region and most of the interesting places are within an hour's drive from Mostar. Listed here are not only the most convenient attractions, but also a few off-the-beaten-track treasures.

BLAGAJ

Blagaj's highlights are the Buna Spring and the adjacent Ottoman house/ monastery. The spring is amazing. It flows out of a 200m cliff wall and single-handedly creates the Buna River. Unsurprisingly, the Ottoman sultan was impressed, and ordered a **tekija** to be built right next to it. This 16th century house/monastery was built for the Dervish cults and is still one of the most mystical places in all of Bosnia and Herzegovina. It is open to visitors all year round and serves cold drinks, tea and Turkish coffee in a beautiful garden overlooking the source of the River Buna. Entrance to the house is only 2KM. You must wear long trousers to enter the house and women are given a shawl to cover their heads. The house tour is self-guided and is most interesting for its woodwork and well-preserved oldstyle sitting and prayer rooms. There are plenty of quality handmade souvenirs and Islamic music that you can buy at the entrance. Although this has turned from a monastery into a tourist attraction, it managed to keep a most peaceful and laidback ambience. There is a small trail across the wooden footbridge that leads almost directly to the cave where the Buna exits. From there, you can capture the whole tekija house for a photo.

Blagaj's old town is worth taking a walk through. This lazy Herzegovinian town moves at a slow pace and many of its old structures are reminiscent of Ottoman days. A newly built heritage trail around the town is a rather pleasant 30-45 minute walk starting at the Tekija-Dervish House. The **Velagić House** was built in 17th century and is a beautiful example of Ottoman stone masonry. In the vicinity are also old flourmills that the strong Buna powered. Recently, the family has decided to open one part of the housing complex to visitors. The houses and the grounds are truly remarkable and one of the most peaceful oasis for a home that I have ever visited. One of the owners, a young man named Almir Milavić, speaks perfect French and very good English. He will gladly give you a tour and afterwards you can

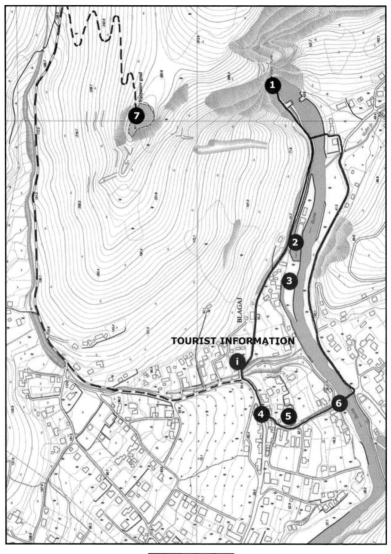

BLAGAJ

1   Vrelo Bune (Buna Springs) and the Tekija-Dervish Monastery
2   Norfish fishfarm and restaurant
3   Ottoman era Velagić Estate and mills - 16th century
4   Čaršija - Blagaj's Old Town
5   Sultan Sulejman Džamija / Mosque, built in 1520
6   Karađoz-begova ćuprija from 1570
7   The fort of Herceg Stjepan

enjoy a coffee or tea on the cool banks of the Buna River.

Just a short walk from the Tekija house is the **Norfish restaurant**. Here you can handpick your choice of fresh trout from the cold waters of the Buna (it maintains a constant temperature of 10°C). The food is excellent and they serve traditional meat dishes as well as trout. With wine, a hearty meal will cost around 20KM or less. Pass the restaurant back towards town in the old čaršija, and you'll see the **Sultan Sulejman Mosque** from 1520 and the beautiful **Ottoman Karađoz-begova ćuprija** built in 1570 over the Buna River. The well kept paved trail then follows the Buna back to its source on the other side and to great spots for photographing the spring and the Tekija House.

If you are in for a bit of hiking, you could walk to the **fortress of Herceg Stjepan,** who ruled Hum (present-day Herzegovina) in the Middle Ages. This fort was originally an Illyrian tribe settlement that was later reinforced by the Roman invaders, further fortified by the ruling Bosnian state and significantly expanded with the arrival of the Ottomans. Atop the high cliffs, this fort is accessible by a winding trail that takes about an hour to walk. It has not been conserved but many of its high walls are still intact. It is a great place for a view of the **Neretva Valley** and an ideal picnic spot. The trail is not marked but easy to find. There are no guides or entrance fees to the fort.

If the Buna inspires you to stay overnight there is a lovely motel, **Pansion Ada** (036 572 500 or 061 106 206). It has a restaurant and bar and, being situated right on the Buna River, is a perfect solution for hot summer nights. It is located at the entrance to Blagaj and clearly signposted.

To get to Blagaj, take bus number 10 from the Mostar central station.

Motel Sunce

Among the rich tourist destinations of Herzegovina this is one of the least-known gems. The Podveležje plateau rests between the towering peaks of Velež Mountain and the city of Mostar. For centuries it has been home to highland shepherds and a traditional way of life. The landscape is harsh arid karst dotted with small forests of beech and oak trees. Podveležje has even more sunny days than Mostar. Situated 700m above sea level it is a pleasant escape during the hot summer nights and an ideal place for walking, mountain biking, medicinal herb picking and challenging treks to Velež's highest peak at 1,980m. Here one can witness many of the old methods of traditional life including sheepshearing, milk, cheese and butter production, honey-making, meat drying and wool sewing. There are miles of asphalted roads across the plateau with almost no traffic. 6km off the main road to Nevesinje from Mostar, marked with signs starting from the turnoff to Blagaj on the M-17, is the small village of Smajkići and the eco-motel Sunce. The owner can arrange walks, hikes and herb picking on the spot and local guides can take you to Velež's peaks. It serves traditional, organic Herzegovinian meals in one of the most peaceful settings on earth - do try the house specialities of grilled lamb, pita baked under the sać (see Traditional Foods) and home-made soup. The honey and jam served with home-baked bread at breakfast is worth the bargain price of 45KM for accommodation, breakfast, lunch and dinner. Evenings on Podveležje are a welcome break from the summer heat and the sunsets will leave a lasting impression. Sunce serves many domestic Herzegovinian wines ... the author recommends Stankela white wine! Local buses (number 16) run from the main bus station in Mostar six times per day.

DREŽNICA

The settlement of Drežnica sits humbly under the massive rock faces of **Čabulja and Čvrsnica Mountains**. Only 20km north of Mostar, it is easily accessed just off the M-17 towards Sarajevo. The **River Drežanka** cuts through the deep valley and 12 canyons feed the Drežanka along its 18km of stunning terrain. It is an ideal car ride for the picturesque views and awe-inspiring canyons. The deeper you travel into the canyon, the further back in time you feel you've gone. The tiny villages that dot the mountainside are remnants of old world Europe and a traditional way of life. See the Jablanica section for more details.

DIVA GRABOVICA

If you're a hiker or nature lover, just a glimpse of this valley will tempt you to extend your trip. Diva Grabovica is the natural boundary between the Mediterranean and continental climates. Its position has produced an eco-system unlike any other found in Bosnia and Herzegovina. In the tiny village of Diva Grabovica there are no more than ten homes, and, like needles in a haystack, they sit in a green valley surrounded by a great wall of limestone rock that towers 2,000m above. For more details see the Jablanica section of this guide book.

MEĐUGORJE

The story of Međugorje is well known to most Catholics. Ever since six teenagers had a vision of the Mother Mary, Queen of Peace, this sleepy Herzegovina village has become the second largest Catholic pilgrimage site in the world. There has been much controversy over the legitimacy of the visions, so much so that the Pope has not recognized it as an official pilgrimage site. Nonetheless, millions of faithful Catholics from all over the world visit this sacred spot, and the many amazing accounts suggest that miracles are a regular occurrence here.

Getting there

If there is anywhere in Herzegovina that you can reach day or night it is most certainly Međugorje. There are half a dozen daily buses to Međugorje from Mostar, starting at 06.30 in the morning and running until at least 19.00. Dubrovnik, Split, Makarska and Zagreb all have regular buses to Međugorje as well.

Tourist information

Međugorje is well organized. Its Tourist Office is located on Mala livada (tel/fax: 036 651 011; email: tzm-medjugorje@tel.net.ba; web: www.tel.net.ba/tzm-medjugorje). For good independent guides for both Međugorje and Herzegovina you can contact Dragan Zovko (tel: 063-323-987) or Silvije Kraljević (tel: 061-516-280; email: silvijek@hotmail.com). They both speak perfect English and know the entire region extremely well.

Travel Agencies in Međugorje

If you are looking for a travel agency for accommodation, transport or guides:

G-tour Međugorje; tel: 036 650 126; fax: 036 650 156; email: davor@globtour-medjugorje.com; web: www.globtour-medjugorje.com. They have a lot of experience with visitors from the UK and the United States.

Paddy Travel Glavna ulica bb; tel/fax: 036 650 482; email: paddy@tel.net.ba; web: www.paddy-travel.com. This is an Irish/Herzegovinian venture that deals with accommodation and bus charters from Ireland and the UK.

Glob Tour; Međugorje bb; tel: 036 651 393, 651 593, 651 693; e-mail: globtour@globtour.com, globtour@tel.net.ba; web: www.globtour.com

Goya Tours; Bijakovića bb; tel/fax: 036 651 700; tel: 036 650 061 e-mail: oli@goyatours.com; web: www.goyatours.com

VOX Tours; Međugorje bb; tel/fax: 036 650 771; e-mail: vox.tours@tel.net.ba; web: www.vox-tours.net

Atlas Ambasador Hotel Ero; tel: 036 318 771

Global; Međugorje bb; tel: 036 651 501, 651 489; e-mail: ok@global-medjugorje.com; web: www.global-medjugorje.com

Grace Travel Bijakovići bb; tel: 036 651 311; e-mail: gracetravel@tel.net.ba

Where to stay

The accommodation standards in Međugorje and Bijakovići are very high and there are too many possibilities to even attempt to put in this guide. Knocking on any door advertising rooms is cheaper than going through a travel agency. Most places will give discounts to groups but it is always good to contact ahead of time to be sure. Međugorje and Bijakovići are the two villages that together form the pilgrimage site. They are very close to each other and can, for all practical purposes, be considered one area. I've listed just a few of the better places:

Hotels

Hotel Pax Bijakovići bb, 036 651 604; fax: 036 650 874; email: pax@tel.net.ba; www.pax.tel.net.ba. This hotel is quite a nice one located just 300m from the church St. Jacob and 1 km from the Apparition Hill. It has 70 rooms. All rooms have bathroom and central heating. The restaurant seats over 300.

Hotel Internacional is located in the very centre of this sacred town. Hotel International offers you the peace of prayer and the excitement of the unknown and the unexpected, as well as any service that can be expected from a hotel in any of the world's capitals. The hotel has a capacity of about 60.

Hotel Annamaria, Bijakovići bb; tel: 036 651 512; fax: 036 651 023; email: hotel.am@tel.net.ba; web: www.tel.net.ba/hotel.am. This medium-sized hotel (it has some 100 beds) does not only have the standard facilities including, in the case of Međugorje, a prayer room, but also the modern private clinic of Dr. Radoslav Lončar.

Hotel Ruža, Međugorje; Bijakovići bb; tel.036 651 822

Hotel Palace, Međugorje; Bijakovići bb; tel. 036 651 061

Motel Matanovi dvori, Međugorje Krstine bb; tel: 036 651 985

Hotel Angels, Međugorje; Tromeđa bb; tel: 036 650 503

Hotel Bim, Međugorje, Sluzanj bb; tel: 036 643 940

Motel Marben, Međugorje, tel: 036 650 910; email: marben@aplus.ba; web: www.marben.aplus.ba

B&B/Pensions

Pansion Toni Međugorje, Put za Krizevac bb; tel: 036 651 238; fax: 036 650 285; email: tonisego@tel.net.ba. Near the main route to Cross Mountain.

Pansion Floria Preko puta crkve; tel: 036 651 525; tel/fax: 036 650 806, email: dvasilj@yahoo.com. This pension is situated 700 m from the St. Jacob Church. The pension has 50 beds in double, triple rooms and 1 suite. Each room has its own bathroom. The restaurant is air conditioned and has 75 seats.

Pansion Palma Crkva sv. Jakova; no phone. This pension is situated right above St. Jacobs Church. It has 48 beds.

Pansion Ero - The pension is situated in Međugorje, 200 m away from St. Jacob Church. It has accommodation for 65 persons. There is also a restaurant and a coffee bar attached to it.

Pansion Mir Međugorje, tel: 036 651 166; fax: 036 651 441; email: filip.kozina@tel.net.ba

Pansion Nada Međugorje, tel: 036 651 786

Pansion Marin Međugorje, Krstina bb; tel: 036 651 324

Pansion Vila Andrea Međugorje, Krstina bb; tel: 036 651 157

The list goes on and on. With 17,000 beds available you shouldn't have too much trouble finding a place other than at Christmas and Easter.

Where to eat

There is no shortage of good restaurants in Međugorje or Bijakovići. Most hotels and pensions have restaurants with good menus in at least three languages (and always English). A local favorite is just to the right of the church and is owned by a very nice gentleman from Mostar named Krešo. **Colombo's** has gone out of their way to give you the best of both worlds - they serve many dishes that are close to home for Western guests and also offer a good selection of traditional dishes for those looking for a more local flavor. It is right on the main strip and by no means a quite oasis ideal for contemplating God, but nonetheless I am quite sure almost anyone visiting Međugorje visits Colombo's at least once. **Vinarija Stankela** in Bijakovići is the home of the delicious wine I've been raving about. The restaurant is on the same level and specializes in local and Dalmatian dishes and the wine straight out of the wooden barrel makes it taste just that much better. **Restoran Coco** in Međugorje is also a nice spot for good food and wine. You can also check out **Viktor's Restaurant** for some good eatin'. They speak excellent English, the menu is in nine languages and you will always get fast and friendly service. They local wine list is also quite good. **Galija Restoran** has a good selection of seafood and is considered one of the best places in town. **Titanic** right next to Viktor's is a good place for local traditional dishes.

What to see and do

In 1981 six teenagers were playing together in the hills between the villages of Međugorje and Bijakovići. It was on this barren hillside that Mother Mary appeared and spoke to them. When the children told their parents the first reaction was skepticism. The apparitions, however, did not cease. She appeared again and again and soon made believers out of even the most vocal of critics. Since then it is estimated that over 15 million people have visited this tiny place. The Virgin Mary is said to still appear every day but only to one of the teenagers.

A blue cross marks the bare mountain, now called **Apparition Hill**, where the children first saw her. A well-worn footpath on **Cross Mountain**, lined with Stations of the Cross, has been trekked by visitors from every corner of the globe. Many make the trek barefoot. The large cross planted on top of the hill is said to have been built to celebrate the 1,900th anniversary of the death of Christ but it is more likely that it was built in 1934 to keep away the plague that had devastated several areas in the region.

The village of Međugorje has become quite commercialized. It has the capacity to receive tens of thousands of guests at any given moment and the once dead main street has turned into a souvenir shop bazaar. Crosses, rosaries, statues, pictures, posters, jewellery - you name it, it's there. Almost every house provides good quality private accommodation. It is easy to find internet connections, good information, guides in most European languages, and probably the best general service in the country. The main church, **St James**, is in the middle of town. Whether or not there is a mass service, the square around the church is bound to have people sitting, praying and contemplating. One of the Franciscan priests that have been involved in Međugorje's metamorphosis has been **Fra Jozo Zovko** from **Široki Brijeg**. It is said he gives moving and magical sermons that attract thousands to his church in Široki Brijeg, only a few kilometers from Međugorje (see Široki Brijeg section).

Just up the road is the even smaller village of **Bijakovići.** Despite the massive influx of tourists and pilgrims it has managed to maintain much of its original old Herzegovinian style, and you can find accommodation in many of the traditional stone homes. The tradition of winemaking goes back much further than the apparition. Stankela wine from Bijakovići has won numerous international awards and on the premises of the vineyards is a bed and breakfast. Tours of the cellars are possible.

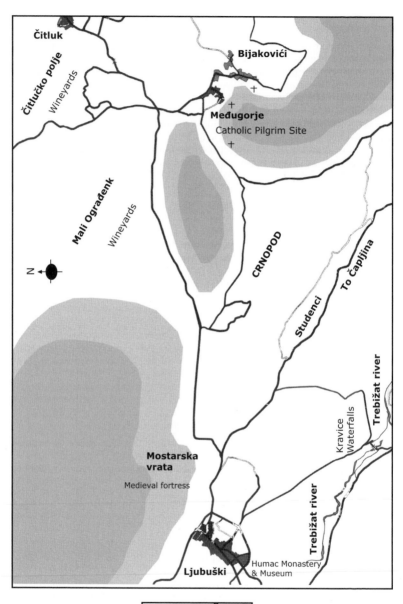

LJUBUŠKI

There is another winemaking community just a few kilometers up the road from Meðugorje (see map). **Čitluk** is known for its good quality žilavka and blatina grapes. The road leading to Čitluk is lined on both sides with rolling hills of vineyards. Aside from its winemaking tradition, Čitluk has always been an ideal place for growing tobacco. If you have a car, take any of the small side roads through the countryside. Seeing the tobacco drying in front of traditional homes and the local villagers working the vineyards is a truly authentic glimpse into the past.

The village of **Surmanci** is only 6 kilometers from Meðugorje – it is a wonderful small village on the western banks of the Neretva. There is a seasonal restaurant run by the Cikola family that serves excellent trout and has a wonderful natural ambiance. The wine and spirits are homemade and they serve frogs and escargot.

AROUND MEÐUGORJE

LJUBUŠKI

Ljubuški is another ancient settlement in the vast rocky hills of western Herzegovina. The ruling family of the medieval Bosnian state expanded their reign to this region and the remains of their **old fort** still jut out of the hill overlooking the **Trebižat River** valley.

Both the Illyrians and the Romans settled the lands along the Trebižat before the Slavs settled in this part of world. The oldest museum in the country, established in 1884, is at the **Humac Franciscan Monastery** (built in 1869) just outside the town of Ljubuški. The **Humac Museum** hosts one of the finest collections of ancient relics, all found in the vicinity of the monastery. The oldest script ever found in the territory of Bosnia and Herzegovina, the Humačka ploča, is exhibited here. This stone-carved slate written in Glagolithic is said to date back to the 10th century. The museum has a significant collection of relics from the Roman settlements including jewellery, weapons, helmets and hand carved tombstones. Many of the excavated items come from the ruins of a Roman military camp, **Bigeste,** near the monastery. This quaint museum is an interesting stop.

The village of **Vitina** is a bit off the beaten path to the north of Ljubuški. There is a great traditional restaurant at the source of the River Vrioštice and sitting there is a good way to beat the summer heat. **Kočuša Waterfall,** a mini version of Kravica in Veljaci, is situated just a few minutes outside of Vitina.

Ljubuški and the surrounding area are also famous for winemaking, the best being **Gangaš.** Stop at **Konoba** and **Restaurant Ramljak** (Josipa bana Jelačića bb) for a local or Dalmatian specialty with a fine bottle of local Gangaš. The pršut, the local equivalent to prosciutto from Italy, is said to be some of the best around. Ljubuški has drastically expanded in size over the past decade and has a decent selection of good restaurants and café's. **Motel-restaurant Most** on Teskera 1 has good food and accommodation. **Avantgarde** on the main strip has great pizzas.

KRAVICA WATERFALLS

The gem of this region is the crystal-clear water of the Trebižat River. Southeast of Ljubuški are the Kravica Waterfalls. Stretching over 100m across and tumbling down 25m, Kravica is one of the largest waterfalls in Herzegovina and certainly the most impressive one. The waterfalls have a natural pool dug out at the base of the falls by the constant rush of water. It is a favorite local swimming hole with picnic area, café and even a place to pitch a tent if you like. The best time of year for visiting is springtime when the waterfall is at its fullest and the arid landscape turns a bright green. During the season there are a few café's near the picnic area and I've never heard of any campers getting turned away. There are some great spots to pitch a tent. Be careful with campfires and always follow a "leave no trace" policy (even if there are obviously many who don't).

ŠIROKI BRIJEG

The best way to find an interesting spot in or around Široki Brijeg is to follow the ever-present water to its source. Both life and leisure completely depend on it. **Mostarsko blato** is the large flood basin to the east of Široki Brijeg. In the rainy season this lush valley floods as the **Lištica River** jumps her banks. The little villages dotting the valley are still preserved in the old style. The traditional **old mills** used over the centuries to grind wheat into flour can still be seen at the source of the Lištica River.

The old Franciscan church at **Cerigaj** is one of the few remaining old Catholic structures in this part of Herzegovina. More alive, the **Franciscan monastery** on top of the hill is open to guests and often receives visitors from Međugorje. Fra Jozo Zovko attracts thousands of worshippers to his moving sermons. He speaks only in Croatian but the masses are translated into several languages each week. The statue near the main parking lot of the church is dedicated to **Fra Didak Buntić**. During the First World War there was a great famine in the region and Fra Buntic apparently marched thousands of children north to Slavonia in Croatia where they were saved from the famine.

GRUDE

The **Ravlića Caves** near the springs of the Trebižat have uncovered evidence that human life has existed here since Neolithic times. That is not surprising, as the Trebižat River makes this area a fertile oasis amid the harsh landscape of western Herzegovina. In the green valley along the Trebižat, tobacco and grapes are grown, and Grude is yet another winemaking centre.

The old mills and waterfalls at **Peć Mlini** give a feel for how things used to be. Krenica Lake, north of Grude, can be found on most maps and is a pleasant place to get away for a picnic or a swim. **Motel Kiwi** (039 674 079) in Ružići is a nice, modern place if you decide to hang about and explore the caves.

As border crossings in this area are generally efficient, it is worth a border crossing to **Imotski** in Croatia for a quick excursion to **Modro** and **Crveno lakes**. Crveno Lake is no less than a natural phenomenon - the lake sits in a 296m natural crater. Karst sinkholes in this region are not uncommon but this is truly a sight to see.

ČAPLJINA

Čapljina is a border town, centrally located between Mostar to the north and the Adriatic Sea to the south. Međugorje and Ljubuški are less than 20km to the west, and Stolac is less than half an hour's drive to the east. This town on the west bank of the Neretva River was once the home of what is thought to be the largest Roman military camp in the region. **Mogorjelo** was built at the end of the 3rd century and two basilicas were added some time in the 5th century. It makes for an interesting excursion. If you really like it, you might want to continue to the ancient settlement of **Gabela**, further towards the border with Croatia. It is mentioned for the first time in the second half of the 15th century and is believed to have been a significant settlement long before that.

But most people come here for a canoe safari on the Trebižat River. The launching spot for the canoes is a bit hard to find but the **Villa Rustica** next to (or actually a part of) Mogorjelo can provide information on how to get there. Stop there even if you don't need directions: Rustica is one of the best restaurants in the country, with excellent food and a cool, breezy ambiance. I've yet to try any dish I didn't like and the service is attentive and friendly.

The owner of Villa Rustica (Marinko Previšić; tel: 063 323 515) could organise your canoe safari for 38KM per person (or more if your group is small). His season starts in June. The safari is a 10km, five-hour journey down the Trebižat River southeast of Kravica Waterfalls. It normally starts between 10 and 11.00. The canoeing is not difficult, with a calm river and only a few small (and fun) cascades to conquer. Marinko will accept children age ten and above. The water is cold and refreshing if you do happen to fall in. Midway through the journey you'll stop for a BBQ lunch prepared by your guide's team. The food is great and Marinko even caters for vegetarians.

If you need accommodation after a long day on the river and exploring the sites in Čapljina, you'll be happy with **Hotel J&B** on Mostarska 15 (036 805 382), a new hotel with modern facilities. Motel Karaotok (addressed under Hutovo blato in this guide) is also very close to Čapljina and has a fantastic natural setting on the river and lake.

POČITELJ

A great D-tour on your way to the coast or to Hutovo blato, this quaint oriental-style town is located about half an hour's drive from Mostar, less than 30km south on the M-17 road towards the Adriatic. This unique settlement, listed as a UNESCO heritage site, was heavily damaged during and sadly even after the war, but recent reconstruction has returned the town to its original form. Besides its stunning oriental architecture and Ottoman feel, Počitelj hosts the longest operating art colony in southeast Europe. Artists from around the world gather here to paint, among other things but importantly, the shiny red pomegranates and figs that grow in abundance on the hills of Počitelj.

The **Dadži-Alija Mosque** has been reconstructed as well as the **Sisman-Ibrahimpašina medresa** and the **Gavran Kapetanović House**, all of which are open to visitors. The most striking object in Počitelj is the **Sahat-kula**, a silo-shaped fort that towers from the top of the hill above

the town. It housed watchmen and military to guard against possible invasion from the Neretva Valley. It is open, but there are no signs to point you
in the right direction through the maze of winding stone steps.

Should the amazing architecture and authentic Ottoman feel entice
you enough to stay the night, **Motel Jelčić** (036 826 165) has nice, clean
rooms for a reasonable price. Alternatively, you could ask around in the old
town, as there may be a few private homes that rent out rooms to guests
during the season. An early morning in Počitelj, sipping a coffee up on the
hill and listening to the birds chirp around the fig trees, is most inspiring.

To get there take bus number 41 from Mostar to Čapljina via Počitelj.

HUTOVO BLATO

Hutovo blato Bird Reserve is marshland, created by the underground aquifer system of the Krupa River. It is fed from the limestone massif of **Ostrvo**
that divides the **Deransko** and **Svitavsko** lakes. *The International Council
for Bird Protection* placed this reserve on the list of important bird habitats,
and did so for good reasons: this reserve is the largest of its kind in this
part of Europe, in terms of both size and diversity. It is home to over 240
types of migratory birds and dozens that make their permanent home in
these sub-Mediterranean wetlands surrounding **Deransko Lake**. In the
migration season, tens of thousands of birds fill this lake and its surroundings. The best way to see these birds is to rent a boat, which can be done
from the reserve's only hotel. Per hour, these 'barcos' cost 40KM (for up to
six persons), 60KM (for up to ten persons) or 100KM (for ten to 15 persons). They come with a professional biologist guide, who speaks English
and takes an additional 30KM.

The reserve provides a unique oasis amongst the harsh arid karst of
western Herzegovina. Teeming with freshwater fish, wild duck, geese, coots,
hawks, herons, pheasants, wild boar and wild horses, it accommodates
birdwatchers, nature lovers and families with children alike. For the latter,
there is a very short but cute educational walk that starts from the hotel.

Hutovo blato is located only 5km from the city of Čapljina and is marked
with clear signs on the M-17. There is no entrance fee to the park and it is
open all year round. It also has a picnic area, restaurant/café and a newly
renovated hotel (Karaotok Hotel; tel: 036 814 990; email:
nikola.zovko.karaotok@tel.net.ba).

NEUM

The **Adriatic Sea** from Split to Dubrovnik is gorgeous, very clean, and
includes 22km of Bosnia and Herzegovina. The closed bay at Neum is protected from the strong open sea winds by the **Pelješac Peninsula**, and
wonderfully calm.

Most of the town was built during Yugoslav times as an isolated retreat
for the communist elite. Its face has changed drastically since then with the
new construction of Dalmatian stone homes and more modern architecture. The large hotels from the socialist era appear somewhat awkward in
this serene setting.

Tourism has returned to this place and scuba-diving, parasailing, boating
and jet skiing can all readily be arranged in any of the major hotels. It all

costs a little less than what it costs in Croatia. During the season, it is wise to book in advance.

Getting there and around

The only land connection Neum has to Bosnia and Herzegovina is through the hinterlands towards Hutovo where a narrow two-lane road winds through the hills. To go to Neum via the main coastal road you must first enter Croatia (at the **Metković** border crossing if coming from Mostar), then re-enter Bosnia and Herzegovina after the tourist settlement of **Klek**. Neum is 8km from the border crossing. After 22km you'll be crossing back into Croatia heading towards Dubrovnik. Generally, none of these border crossings will cost you any time.

Where to stay

The large hotels are like cities within themselves, offering almost everything you might need within the hotel compound. The pensions and bed and breakfasts around town are of equal quality and certainly provide more privacy. The major hotels are:

Hotel Stella Tel: 036 880 055; fax: 036 880 051; email: info@stella-neum.com; web: www.stella-neum.com. Stella has a great panoramic view of the bay, easy access to the beach and a beautiful terrace restaurant. The rooms are quite nice and all have AC, phone, and satellite TV. The restaurant, as is the norm in Neum, serves Dalmatian and local specialties and has a great local wine list.

Hotel Zenit Tel: 036 880 139; fax: 036 880 140. This is the most spacious hotel in Neum, with a 340-bed capacity and a large beach on the premises. The rooms are simple but do the job if you plan on being at the beach all day. There is an indoor swimming pool, sauna, playground, tennis courts and even a small bowling alley. Excursions by boat or coach can be organized to other seaside towns and to Herzegovina.

Hotel Sunce Tel: 036 880 033/034/035; fax: 036 880 065; email: uprava@hotel-sunce.com; web: www.hotel-sunce.com. Right on the beach in the centre of Neum with a capacity of 400, it offers single and double rooms as well as apartments. There is a dentist, hairdresser, boutique, billiards and aperitif bar on the premises. In addition there is a restaurant, tavern, beer and wine cellar, pastry shop and pizzeria.

Hotel Neum Tel: 036 880 222; fax: 036 880 077; email: hotel.neum@tel.net.ba; web: www.hotel-neum.com. The largest of them all with 380 rooms available. The rooms don't have TV or AC and are highly reminiscent of socialist days. There is a large pool and direct access to the beach via lifts in the hotel.

Private accommodation is available in almost every home in Neum. Just to name a few...

Vila Matić Tel/fax: 036 880 453; email: villa.matic@max.net.ba; web: www.i-reception.net/matic

Vila Nova Tel/fax: 036 880 245; email: nova@tzneum.com; web: www.tzneum.com/nova. This one of the finest small pensions directly on the beach. They rent rooms and apartments (apartments have kitchens)

for 80KM during the season and half the price in the off-season. The rooms all have AC and there is a restaurant in the pension.

Vila Barbara Tel: 036 880 026. Next door and offering similar accommodation minus the kitchen in each apartment.

Motel More Jadranska turistička magistrala bb; tel: 036 880 677.

Where to eat

All the hotels have restaurants and most of the package deals include full board. If you get out and go for a meal in a more intimate and authentic setting, you'll find many excellent restaurants with Dalmatian and Herzegovina specialties on the menu. If you just want a pizza and a football match on TV, you'll easily find one of Neum's local joints.

Restoran Hum is Neum's finest restaurant, serving traditional Dalmatian meals and wines. Extra care goes into food preparation and the place is well known for its high quality and fresh seafood. Prices are mid-ranged, service is great – you won't be disappointed.

Restoran-picerija Laguna Kralja Tomislava 26. An inexpensive place for a good pizza and a chilled atmosphere.

Restoran Bonaca Kralja Tomislava bb. A classier restaurant with good seafood dishes and Dalmatian wine. Main courses will cost you 10-25KM depending on the type of fish and the season.

Restoran El Poncho Zagrebačka 7. This restaurant does not offer Spanish or Mexican food as the name may suggest, but traditional specialties of seafood and meat, almost always grilled and served with domestic wine.

What to see and do

Neum is a holiday resort town. There is not much on the cultural 'to do' list but there is plenty of fun in the sun on offer. Besides swimming and sunbathing, there are boats for rent at several places on the beach. From Neum you can jump on the excursion boats that travel up and down the Adriatic coastline. Scuba diving is relatively inexpensive compared to Croatia and other western Mediterranean countries. Jet skis and water skiing are also organized from beachside rental outlets. **Dubrovnik** is only an hour's drive from Neum, and the peninsula of Pelješac is a stone's throw away.

From Orebić on Pelješac you can catch a ferry to the beautiful island of Korčula. In the hinterland behind Neum is the village of **Hutovo** and the ancient ruins of **Hadžibegova kula Fortress,** used by the Ottomans to defend their western front. The holy site of **Svetište Kraljica mira** is a shrine to the Queen of Peace in **Hrasno.** It has more local significance but those who have come on a pilgrimage often pay a visit to this tiny hinterland shrine. Hutovo blato, Ljubuški and Međugorje are all within an hour's drive of Neum for day trips, with Mostar only being a little further.

STOLAC

This quaint, sunny southern town full of striking Ottoman architecture is a true playground for those intrigued by anthropology, archaeology and history. The area has been settled for at least 15,000 years as evidenced by the markings in **Badanj Cave**, which experts have dated 12000-16000 BC.

Throughout its long history, Stolac has been an outstandingly cultured town. No other town in Bosnia and Herzegovina has produced such a rich array of intellectuals, artists, poets and leaders. Strolling through Stolac to the sound of the rushing Bregava and the many songbirds, it is easy to imagine the inspiration felt by its many generations of extraordinary personalities.

The town saw significant damage in the recent war. After a short siege by the Bosnian Serb army in 1992 and continued shelling into 1993, the Croat-Bosniac alliance fell apart and the Croatian Defense Council expelled or imprisoned most of the Bosniac inhabitants. Shortly afterwards most of the town's Ottoman heritage and many of its Bosniac homes were destroyed. Stolac is still a long way from peace and harmony, but by now much of its oriental flavor has been restored and some of the families offer bed and breakfast facilities. It's a great place to stroll around, eat figs, drink the tasty local wine, or dig into one of those delicious pomegranates that grow in every yard. It's also a good base from which to explore the region by bicycle.

The town has a sleepy, Mediterranean air to it and is lined with café's along the crystal-clear **Bregava River**. The Bregava is a favorite spot for youths to swim and dive and one will often find most of the town near the water during the hot and dry summers. The centre enjoys lush trees and foliage, with unique pines darting into the skyline near the ancient old town fortress of **Vidoška** (built in the 14th century).

The Bregava has made Stolac and the surrounding region (called **Dubrava**) one of the most fertile areas in the country. Vegetables and fruit from here seem to taste just that bit better. In the nearby village of **Domanovići,** red and white Doman wine and a new sparkling wine are all produced from the harvests of the local vineyards. They are great and inexpensive wines: Doman can be found in the shops for a mere 5-6KM a bottle.

At the northern entrance to the city is the country's oldest necropolis, **Radimlja.** There are 122 medieval tombstones marked with the unique carvings of 13-15th-century Slavic worshippers of the Bosnian Church. They fascinated the famous poet Mak Dizdar. *Over the stones, smoke drifts once more on the wind. Under the stones, the chosen sleep. But the day they shall wake is at hand.* Buybook in the old town of Mostar has the English language translation of his 'stone sleeper' for sale at over 50 euros.

Although much of the oriental architecture and many Islamic structures were destroyed, several trademark Ottoman bridges remain. The **Inat ćuprija** was built in the mid 17th century and still stands in the middle of town. The **Podgradska ćuprija** was built over half a century before the Inat ćuprija. The construction of the **Begovska ćuprija** was finished at the beginning of the 19th century.

OŠANIĆI

Not far from Stolac is the oldest remaining human settlement in Bosnia and Herzegovina. The Daorsi tribe is said to have lived in these parts over 4,000 years ago. Remnants of Hellenistic art and design have suggested that at least some elements of the Hellenistic civilization reached this far north. Near the small village of Ošanići is the 'Herzegovina Stonehenge' whose massive cyclopean walls are hidden in the thorny brush above Stolac and the Bregava. It may be difficult to find but it's a worthwhile adventure to admire the ingenuity in creating a structure of this magnitude four millennia ago! **The Church of St Peter and Paul** from the year 1500 managed to escape the systematic destruction of sacred buildings in and around Stolac, and remains intact and worth a visit.

TREBINJE

Trebinje ranks with Mostar and Stolac in terms of beauty. It is the southernmost city in Bosnia and Herzegovina and is only 28km from the famous city of Dubrovnik. This area fortunately escaped the fates of Mostar and Stolac and was not heavily damaged during the war, leaving its old town intact. Many of the Islamic structures were destroyed, however, erasing an important trace of Trebinje's history. Despite its close vicinity to Dubrovnik in Croatia, it is mostly the Serbian and Bosnian cultures that have shaped this town. The town today has a mainly Serb population.

There is barely a town in Herzegovina that was not erected alongside a freshwater river. Trebinje is no exception: its old town lines the banks of the Trebišnjica River that flows through the heart of the city. The river and the city have always been known for the enormous old mills treading the Trebišnjica. Although they are not fully functional today, they remain a symbol of Herzegovina's not-so-distant past when everything was directly connected to the power of nature. In Trebinje, that power of nature was bigger before the river had been curtailed by the Grančarevo dam, some 15 km north-east from Trebinje. This dam was bound to swallow the **Arslanagić Bridge**. To save this beautiful example of Ottoman stone bridge building, it was taken, stone by stone, from a village seven kilometers up the river, and rebuilt in downtown Trebinje.

Klobuk is the large fortress in Trebinje. It is assumed to date from the 9th century and is believed that the Slovenian princes of Krajina - Pavlimir and Tešimir were buried here. Since the 12th century it controlled the Nemanjić region until, in 1377, Klobuk became part of the expanded Bosnian state.

If you like roughing it, the religious monuments covered in the box below are interesting places to visit. Don't expect too much by ways of information or assistance as tourism development has not reached this part of the world. There is little in the way of information on these sites, and you might find it difficult to even find them. The same lack of development typifies the **Bilećka Lake** and **Bileća**. The first is a large artificial lake and a great fishing spot. The area is poorly marked and there is no boat rental for fishermen. The second is a small town. There is nothing much to see or do in it, but historically this place is of some importance. Bileća was the site of the earliest battles with the Ottomans in the 1380s, which repelled the Ottoman invasion of Herzegovina for almost a century. Roman mosaics and Bronze Age gravesites have been discovered in the countryside near Bileća at **Panik** and **Orah.**

In the region that follows **Popovo polje** towards Ljubinje there is an invisible dividing line. The eastern slopes of the valley are by and large populated by Orthodox Christians, whereas the west side has a large Catholic population. Yet again in Bosnia and Herzegovina, two civilizations meet head to head. In this valley in particular one can witness the old ways of life

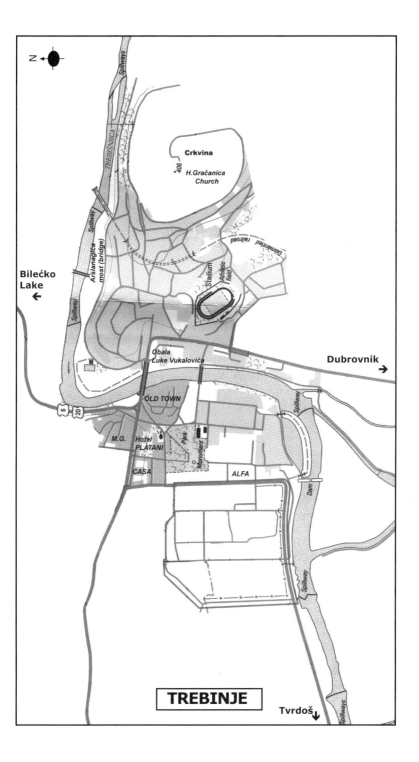

of both these civilizations.

If you decide to stay in Trebinje before heading north to Sutjeska National Park or to Dubrovnik on the coast, there are two good hotels. **Hotel Leotar** (059 261 082)**,** on the southeast side of the river, is the main hotel from the Yugoslav days. It is nice but overpriced. A nicer and cheaper alternative is **Platani Hotel** on Cvijetni Trg 1 (tel: 059 225 134/135). The hotel is small but with pleasant rooms, a restaurant and a café. **M.G. restaurant** (Majke Jugovića 10, 50 meters from Kralja Petra; tel: 059 260 887) is a stylish three-floor place that serves the best food in town. Their portions are large. When coming from Mostar, you can't miss **Alfa restaurant** (Carina bb; tel: 059 223 133) at the beginning of town. The place serves large-sized meat dishes. It has a nice terrace. **Casa** (V. Karadžića 19; tel: 059 270 610) serves Italian dishes in a large garden-with-waterfall in the centre of town. If you're into wine and rakija, go to **Vukoje** at Trebinje's entrance from Bileća (Bezigradska 1; tel: 059 270 370; 065 669 667). Their domestic dishes are nothing special but the owner won several gold medals for his home-made liquors.

Religious monuments in and around Trebinje

There are plenty of religious monuments in and around Trebinje. On **Crkvina hill** protruding from the centre of town is a beautiful church named **Hercegovačka Gračanica**. It is recent but worth visiting as it is an exact - though smaller - copy of 13th century Gračanica Monastery in Kosovo, one of the most exquisite Orthodox buildings ever built. It was built partly to honor Jovan Dučić (1879-1943), one of the greatest Serb poets and writers. In accordance with his testament, his remains were transported from America and reburied in, as he used to call this town, 'his Trebinje'.

Not far from town is the **Trvdoš Orthodox Monastery**, which currently serves as the Episcopal residence after it was moved from Mostar in the recent war. This is where Saint Vasilije – known as the 'Miracle Maker' - started a monastic order in the 17th century. Later, after he had escaped the Ottomans and moved to Montenegro, he built Monastery Ostrog. The latter is built on a huge cliff and Orthodox, Catholics and Muslims all go there believing that the enshrined body of Saint Vasilije still makes miracles work. Trvdoš Orthodox Monastery is not quite *that* spectacular, but certainly worth a visit. It is open to visitors, provided these visitors do not wear shorts, tank tops or sandals.

Monastery Duži is located in the area of Šuma Trebinjska, southwest of Trebinje. It was established after the destruction of Trebinje Monastery in 1694, and soon became the headquarters for the episcope. There is another small stone Orthodox monastery, built in 1514, in **Zavala**. A fourth monastery is **Dobrićevo Monastery.** It dates back to the 15th century and has a stone roof structure that is very characteristic of old Herzegovinian monasteries and churches, both Catholic and Orthodox. The monastery is home to a fresco painting from 1619, an extraordinary work of the most prestigious Serb painter from 17th century, Georgije Mitrofanović.

There is the 16th century Church of Saint Archangel Mihailo in

Aranđelovo and there are three orthodox churches in the village of **Gomiljani,** west of Trebinje. The latter three were damaged heavily in the past war, but one, devoted to St. Gergije (Đurđevića), has several of the fresco paintings still intact.

Taleža, the Church of Saint Sunday, is located in eastern part of Šuma Trebinjska. Its significance lies mostly in its remarkable medieval graveyard with more than 70 stećci (the ancient tombstones of the Bosnian Church), some of which are decorated with motives of crosses and swords with shields. In the close proximity of the church, the antique bronze statue of goddess Dijana was found.

Many other findings were made in the surroundings of **Veličani,** the Church of St. Archangels in Popovo polje. This medieval church was rebuilt in 19th century and its grounds are marked by a necropolis with medieval stećci. Archeological digs have uncovered money, silk lace embroidered in silver and a precious sample of medieval glass which is assumed to be made in one of the Apulija workshops. The findings are now preserved in the Trebinje museum – which unfortunately has irregular working hours and no services in English or any foreign language.

Lastly, there is one mosque. **Osman-pašina džamija** was built in 1726 (some say it's much older), and completely destroyed in 1993. Its reconstruction is nearing completion, and the mosque should be open to visitors by the time this book is for sale.

VJETRENICA CAVE, *by Ivo Lučić*

Vjetrenica cave is in Zavala in the municipality of Ravno, only 25 km from the city of Dubrovnik. The cave is one of the most interesting phenomena of the Dinaric karst, the world's main area of that kind of relief. In addition to the usual attributes and mythology related to caves, Vjetrenica is unique in its structure, natural phenomena and cultural history.

High winds created at the entrance of the cave have attracted interest for thousands of years and Vjetrenica was mentioned in the "Historia Naturalis", the first European encyclopedia by Pliny the Elder, in 77 AD.

Morphologically, Vjetrenica is an extremely developed system of 5800 m of explored channels in several levels. By its origin, it is a sinkhole created by huge amounts of postglacial water finding its way down from Maglić, at the top of Bosnia and Herzegovina, to the sea. Vjetrenica has many constant water flows, lakes, stalactites and stalagmites, huge karst walls created by caving in of the ceiling, etc.

In terms of endemic subterranean species, Vjetrenica it is the second cave in the world with 76 species exclusively adapted to underground conditions. As many as 33 troglobionts were described in Vjetrenica, 12 of them so far spotted in Vjetrenica and nowhere else.

Bones of prehistoric animals were found in Vjetrenica in large numbers. Among them, there was the complete skeleton of a leopard.

There are also reliefs of traditional standing tomb-stones (so-called *stećak*) on the entrance stone of Vjetrenica, and the remnants of walls at the entrance to the cave support the ancient chroniclers' claims there used to be a villa here, with a natural air-conditioning system using the winds from the cave. Bosnian and Croatian ethnography claim that it to be the only such case documented.

For more than a century Vjetrenica has been a tourist attraction, and in 1964 electricity was brought to some 1050m of the cave. All the equipment and archives were completely destroyed in the recent war, but much of the infrastructure has been repaired and the cave is now open to visitors again. Further research has recently begun and it is expected for Vjetrenica to be placed on the UNESCO natural heritage list.

KONJIC

Konjic is attractive far less for its downtown area than for the abundance of natural beauty that surrounds the town. The Neretva River running through the centre and Prenj Mountain hovering behind dominate Konjic. The old town is quite nice to stroll through, although there won't be any signs or tourist information available. The center of town is rather pleasant too, with stunning views in every direction. The main street is often closed to vehicle traffic and is filled with the young and old walking, hanging out in café's or selling their wares along the riverside markets. People in Konjic are very easy going and friendly so feel free to ask someone for directions or to engage in some small talk.

Since the early 1900s, Konjic has come to be known for its woodcarvers. The craft developed a commercial dimension during the Austro-Hungarian occupation in the early 20th century. Before world war II Konjic had a couple of dozen woodcarving businesses, who sold their elaborately-carved heirloom furniture and boxes within the Austro-Hungarian empire and beyond. The **Nikšić** family is one of the few families left that continue to pass on the family trade from father to son. They now have two shops located next to each other: *Brothers Nikšić* and *Rukotvorine* (Varda 2, in the center of Konjic at the intersection for Boračko Lake; tel: 036 725 239 and 036 725 753). Their work is mainly done in European walnut, cherry, and maple. Most of their products are custom-made to order.

Konjic has a few hotels. **Motel Konjic** (Mostarska bb; 036 728 548) is located near the center of the town. It is a relict from socialist times that would more than likely not appease most western travelers. The rooms and food are so-so. For much more comfortable and modern accommodation, go to the new **Hotel Relax** (Ovčari, 036 731 303) in the nearby village of Ovcari. It is on the main road, which isn't too attractive, but the place is definitely a good base if you're in the area for rafting, fishing, or exploring some of the villages. Another good choice is **Motel Vila Palma,** located on the main road right on the bank of the Jablanicko Lake. The motel is new and offers decent rooms and apartments, a beautiful view of the lake, traditionally prepared food and recreational activities such as jet ski (Čelebići, 036 721 263; web: http://jablanicko-jezero.freeservers.com/motel_palma.html).

In the center of Konjic you can eat simple but decent food in restaurant **Neretva** (just off of the bridge on the road Sarajevo-Mostar in the city center), or you can eat a good pizza in **Pizzeria Getzbi** (on a small road across the street from the Konjic High-school). If you have a car, the trip to Restaurant Pećina in the town of Čelebići is well worth the effort (Jablaničko jezero, Čelebići bb; tel: 036 721 229 or 061 154 114; web: http://www.jablanicko-jezero.freeservers.com/restoran_pecina.html). It is a fantastic restaurant built into the side of a cave. The restaurant is situated along a small river that cascades next to the dining terrace. The food and atmosphere are great. The place is sign-posted and not difficult to find: turn left just before the first tunnel you see when driving from Konjic to Mostar.

The epicenter of the Konjic tourism offer is most certainly the area around **Boračko Lake** and the valley of **Glavetičevo**. This partial glacier lake has bungalows, a hotel and camping facilities. Most of the outdoor activities begin from this region: hiking, camping, rafting, kayaking, village tourism, canyoning, mountain biking and even paragliding. You may be a bit disappointed by the seasonal garbage by the lake but the area is stunningly beautiful.

In some areas around the Boračko Lake area there are mines. If you're camping, you're fine. If you want to wander in the surrounding hills, do it with a guide.

The legend of Konjic

Long before the town of Konjic was established as a settlement, there was a small village tucked in the deep valley of Prenj Mountain near Boračko Lake. In this village lived a widow with her two children. One evening a lone traveler appeared in the village, tired and dirty from his journey. He asked several villagers for some food, drink and a place to sleep for the night but, wary of foreigners, they turned him down. He eventually came to the door of the widow and she kindly let him in. As they were eating supper this mysterious vagabond told the widow of an imminent danger that would destroy the village. He warned her to leave at once, at first light, in order to save herself and the children. 'I have come as a messenger, and your fellow villagers have all turned me away.' He instructed her to gather her belongings and take her children on horses over the large mountain to the northwest. The man told her that she would have reached the place where she should make her new home when her horse stopped and dug his hoof into the ground three times.

When the woman awoke the next morning the stranger was gone. She didn't know what to think or believe. She spoke to her neighbors and they laughed at her. She was frightened for her children and wanted to save her neighbors from the impending doom but they would not be convinced. The woman gathered her things and saddled her horses. The journey over the mountain took several days until she reached an open valley near a river. Bowing to the ground her horse dug his hoof into the ground three times. At that moment a large roar rolled down through the valley and the earth shook.

It was here that she settled with her children as the man had instructed her. The little horse had led them to safety and a new life. The settlement of Konjic, meaning little horse, began on this day.

BORAČKO LAKE

Real adventure awaits you over the mountaintop near **Boračko Lake**. Follow the signs for 'rafting' up the long and winding mountain road. It takes about half an hour to travel up and over the mountain. Boračko Glacier Lake is snuggled in between **Prenj, Bjelašnica** and **Visočica mountains**. The lake is open to the public for camping, swimming and BBQs, and a few of the locals have opened bed and breakfasts along the lake. It costs 2KM per person to get into the lake area. The best spot is across the lake by the restaurant where you will find a great freshwater stream and plenty of shade. The **Hotel Borašnica** (036 739 513) has been renovated . It is the only hotel in the area and has very inexpensive half and full board offers, ranging from 25-30 KM. There are also private homes that offer rooms around the lake. Most of the homes are quite nice and cozy and are recommended to those who don't like a hotel atmosphere in nature.

But a sleepy spot in the shade does not provide the adventure to which I referred. This is to be found 5km away where the main road meets the banks of the Neretva again. This whole area is marked as campgrounds for the rafting companies that guide white-water rafting trips down the Neretva Canyon. It's an all-day adventure with plenty of choice of rafting outfits. Some have better gear than others but they all provide you with breakfast and lunch (lunch is usually a BBQ lunch somewhere deep in the canyon) included in the price. The prices are more or less standard and foreigners pay 100KM per person. Some operators give group discounts.

The rafting companies working out of Konjic are:

Europe Rafting Tel: 061 817 209; email: info@raftingeurope.com; web: www.raftingeurope.com. They serve breakfast at the restaurant Stari mlin in Konjic along the Neretva before transporting you for the ride. Europe Rafting has a campground called Tin. Lunch is prepared either in the wilderness or back at the restaurant when the trip is over - your choice.

Hit Tours Konjic Varda 1; tel/fax: 036 725 953. Runs out of Ban Vir near Glavetičevo. They have a small café-bar and camping facilities on site. You can rent kayaks as well and they are a fun and laidback group of guys.

Hit Raft tel: 036 739 221; 061 175 326. This company, near Ban Vir, offers rafting and kayaking with good gear and guides. They also have a beautiful log cabin along the eastern banks of the river

Salihamidžić 036 724 175; are a smaller outfit with good boats and skippers. They have a very nice place in Dejići with excellent food after a long day on the river.

Tajo Raft Konjic/Neretva Rafting: 061 204 260; 061 343 163

Raft Boys: 061 480 061

VISOČICA MOUNTAIN

The isolated string of mountain communities in the highlands of **Visočica** and southern **Bjelašnica** are among the most beautiful in the country. On Visočica Mountain the inhabitants of the many villages of Bijelimići continue to live in the traditional way. Relying mostly on large sheep herds and small farms, the lifestyles have changed very little here over the centuries. The villages are well connected and gravel roads travel far into the high moun-

msko Lake near Prozor

Whitewater rafting on the Neretva River

The ancient lifestyles of the highlanders have seen little
change over the centuries

ing on Prelj Mountain... the Herzegovina Himalayas!

The highlands of Visočica Mountain near Konjic

Fly fishing is a popular sport throughout Herzegovina

tains near the peak of Visočica (Mount Džamija at 1,967m.). This central peak offers staggering views of **Treskavica, Zelengora, Prenj, Velež** and **Bjelašnica mountains** (all over 2,000m).

Visočica escaped the war with little or no damage. Its ancient villages have maintained their original architecture and the old way of highland shepherd life is very much alive. The most interesting of these highland villages are **Grušća and Prebilj** – two villages sitting on the ridge of the Rakitnica. The cheeses and meats from this region are 100% organic and several of the villagers have begun to provide accommodation to hikers, cavers and explorers. Much of this accommodation is very primitive – but very authentic. The villagers live in the main village throughout the winter months and come the first melting snows they move up to **Poljine** – a transitional settlement where they graze their herds for about a month until the higher regions are snow free. They then move into very primitive shelter for the entire length of the summer – living without electricity and water. The traditional huts called *katuni* are enough to provide summer shelter and to store all the milk and meat products. After a season of summer grazing they migrate back down to Poljine for another month before resettling in the lower village for the harsh winter months. This is a truly amazing part of the Visočica highlander experience. Green Visions organizes hikes, camping and village excursions to this remote area (Radnička bb. Sarajevo; tel: 033 717290, 061 213 278; fax: 033 717 291; email: sarajevo@greenvisions.ba; web: www.greenvisions.ba). Ciklo Centar from Ilidža offers mountain bike excursions through the highlands (Hamze Ćelenke 58, Sarajevo; tel: 033 625 243; email: bikeshop@bih.net.ba; web: www.ciklocentar.com) .

SOUTH BJELAŠNICA MOUNTAIN

Across the rugged canyon of Rakitnica is the village of **Dubočani** on the Bjelašnica Mountain side. It is said that the villagers were the last of the followers of the Bosnian Church to convert to Islam after the Ottomans had conquered Herzegovina. There are great hiking trails on **Čepa** ridge towards **Vis** and **Ostro** peaks. The view of the Rakitnica Canyon from this point has been described as one of the most beautiful sights in southeast Europe. Mini-rafting is an adventurous activity in the tight canyon. To cross the entire length of the canyon (26km) takes five or six days with an experienced guide. South Bjelašnica is a beautiful and mine-free area, and hikes around Dubočani, Blace, Džepi and throughout the canyon are all safe for hikers and mountain bikers.

RAKITNICA CANYON

I have quite a dilemma in writing this – let me tell you why. For anyone who loves nature, there are a few times in one's life when you find a place that strikes you as so sacred you either want to keep it to yourself or to simply accept the fact that there are places on this earth that humans simply do not need to go. This is that place – a rugged, and painfully beautiful canyon that stretches between Bjelašnica and Visočica Mountains to southeast of Sarajevo.

The ancient pine and beech tree forests hide all the fairies from us. Bears, wolves, wild boar, pine martens, wild goats all take refuge in this difficult to access canyon. The canyon is 26 km long and feeds the Neretva

River in Herzegovina near Konjic. Rakitnica is a natural wonderland. Hundreds of thousands of years of tectonic shifts have created the steep limestone walls of Visočica and Bjelašnica mountains. The crystal-clear river below is created by the melting snow and the hundreds of underground aquifer systems, making Rakitnica River water potable for the entire length of the canyon. As many as 32 endemic plants, flowers, and trees can be found in this tiny region of the Dinaric Alps.

Regardless of what I write this true force of nature can in no way be relayed to you in print. The life force it has created here hosts dozens of endemic types of plants and flowers. The great limestone walls are home to eagles, falcons and hawks. The river has several types of trout and shellfish. The ridges are lined with tiny villages, ancestors of the last semi-nomadic shepherd tribes to roam these wild lands during Illyrian and Vlach tribal days – which long ago assimilated with newly arrived Slav tribes from the north. The ancient traditions and lifestyles are preserved more so by the power of geographical isolation than of human will.

There are forces here, especially within government, who are blind to the ecological value of the Rakitnica Canyon. They want to build roads and build hydro-electric dams in one of the most pristine and untouched places in all of Europe, further proving the ecologically illiteracy of the leaders of this country. Bosnia and Herzegovina claims to strive towards European integration yet our environmental practices and amount of protected lands are amongst the worst in all of geographical Europe. The vast natural riches also attract European Union partners who willfully and knowingly support the exploitation of the country's water and forest resources. Unfortunately, Bosnians seem to be more than willing to do business with the highest bidders – placing in jeopardy the lush forests and crystal clear rivers that are its greatest resource for a sustainable and healthy future. Hopefully the well intended forces of science, logic and respect for nature will prevail in this saga – if not, Europe certainly loses one its most precious natural resources.

I won't give you instructions on how to get there or what you can see and do. This place is a place of worship – and it should be treated as such. Leave no trace behind if you do go – and rest assured it will leave a lasting trace on you and your impressions of this stunningly beautiful country.

PRENJ MOUNTAIN

Prenj Mountain is accessible from both Konjic and Jablanica. This is the peak of the Herzegovina Himalayas – perhaps the wildest and most challenging mountain in all of Bosnia and Herzegovina. Although there are dozens of fun adventures to be had on Prenj, there is a definite mine risk in several areas in the highlands. You are recommended not to wander on your own. Travel only with a guide through this region when trekking to the many peaks above the 2,000 meter mark, highlighted with the summit to Zelena Glava at 2,155 meters – Prenj's highest peak. See the next section of Jablanica area for more information.

JABLANICA

In the Alps of Austria or Switzerland a place like Jablanica would be a mountain resort town. In Bosnia and Herzegovina, it is a tiny place with little or no developed mountain tourism. Nestled on a terraced plateau below the intimidating peaks of **Prenj** and **Čvrsnica Mountains**, Jablanica teeters between the Mediterranean and continental climates. The Neretva River carves its way through the centre, dividing the massive mountain ranges.

It was at Jablanica that Tito and the partisans, burdened with 4,000 wounded others, won the unlikely **Battle of the Neretva** during World War II. The blown-up bridge that the partisans used to trick the Nazis still hangs from the high cliffs as a reminder of one of the partisans' greatest victories. In addition, there is a war memorial on the peak of Mount Prenj (2,155 meters), dedicated to Tito and the brave men and women who climbed and crossed this cruel - and beautiful – mountain in the most trying of times. The **War Museum** next to the bridge exhibits pictures and tells the story of this famous war episode. An old German bunker on the east side of the river has now been converted into a restaurant and café.

Apart from this famous World War II battle, Jablanica is known for its 'jagnjetinja', lamb meat. The old tradition of roasting sheep over an open fire brought fame to a series of restaurants on the main road (M17) south of the town. Most restaurants are filled day and night and most buses heading south to Mostar or north to Sarajevo stop for a taste of this mouth-watering delicacy. They do, of course, sell other types of food but the craze is definitely for lamb by the kilo. If you are having trouble choosing which restaurant to stop at, **Zdrava voda,** meaning Healthy Water, is certainly one of the nicest (though the toilet facilities are extremely poor) as is **Restoran Jablanica**.

There is only one medium sized hotel in town: **Hotel Jablanica** (tel: 036 753 136), located in the centre of the town on the main road. **Motel Camel** (Pere Bilića 37; tel: 036 752 774) is a smaller and better option. A third place, called Maksumić, is to be avoided because of their horrible environmental record. They dump the remains of your juicy lamb in a massive open pit in Kalajdin Canyon near the Neretva River – exposing locals to stench and disease. When the rains come, the body bits go straight into the river. After many complaints they've still done nothing about it, hiding behind a ridiculous permit the local authorities gave them.

JABLANICA LAKE

North of Jablanica, behind the **Lendava Tunnel,** the **Jablaničko Lake** system begins. This area has developed a tourism niche on the lake. There are several good restaurants, our particular favorite being **Restoran San.** The entire length of the lake is lined with pensions, hotels, private rooms and campgrounds. The lake has some of the best fishing in the country as proved by the locals standing on the side of the road selling their 'catches of the day' - large carp, trout, bass and a few other fish that I haven't been able to translate.

Jablaničko Lake is safe for swimming but don't expect to find lifeguards or any other safety mechanisms in case of an emergency. The campgrounds are as simple as campgrounds can get. **kamp-plaža Miris ljeta** in Ostrožac has camping facilities on the 'beach' of the lake (tel: 036 775 055/195). There is access for campervans and places to pitch a tent but no hook-ups for electricity or water. The place is usually crowded with local people.

Private rooms are easy to find and signs are posted on the road. You might want to bargain a little - a room with a bathroom and shower shouldn't cost more than 25KM per night.

PRENJ - ČVRSNICA - ČABULJA (Proposed National Park)

In the heart of the central Dinaric Alps lies the most imposing set of mountains in the country. Starting on the northern edge of the Mostar county line these ranges climb north all the way to Konjic in northern Herzegovina. Locally this chain is known as the Herzegovina Himalayas. Prenj in particular has seemingly never-ending sharp tooth-like peaks. The lowlands, however, are very accessible and offer one of the most scenic drives in the whole country. This area is known for its many endemic species of wildflowers. It is home to dozens of sleepy Herzegovinian villages where one can find traditional cheese, meats, and the local moonshine called *rakija* (from plumbs) or *loza* (from grapes). Honey and trout are also trademarks of this region and there are usually local villagers selling honey and apple vinegar along the main road (M17).

These mountains offer the best and most challenging hiking in Herzegovina, and it is surprising that this area has seen little in terms of eco-tourism development. Prenj Mountain hosts a wonderful glacier lake named Boračko near the town of Konjic. Not far from there is the Neretva Canyon where several whitewater rafting operators offer an unforgettable rafting adventure through this magical canyon. There are also camping facilities, cafés and fishing sports. More information is provided in the Konjic section.

Prenj Mountain

If you're a hiker it's hard not to gaze up at the massive peaks of Prenj (facing Jablanica) and imagine what the view would be like. It's a bit complicated to find your way up there by yourself, trails are not well marked and there are a few mined areas, so it is advisable to contact the mountain association or an eco-tourism outfit to guide you up. The trek to **Milanova Koliba** (Milan's mountain hut) takes over five hours. From that saddle between **Cetine** and **Izgorila Gruda** peaks, the hike to the top is a little more than an hour away. The view is heavenly! For an easier time on Prenj there is a drivable route from **Bijeli Canyon** off the M-17 south. A long and winding gravel road takes you up to **Glogovo Heights** where you'll drive past highland shepherds and the endangered (and endemic) **Munika black pines.** There is a mountain hut that is often left open for mountaineers. Again, hiking in a region that is mined in some remote areas is not wise. The guide book on the country's mountain hikes "*Forgotten Beauty*" by Matias Gomes, covers all of Prenj's 2,000 meter+ peaks and the routes to get you there! Take that book or find yourself a guide: you'll be happy you did.

Čvrsnica Mountain

The road from Jablanica following the **River Doljanka** towards Doljani leads to another magnificent hiking area on **Čvrsnica Mountain**. There is a new gravel road that climbs to the base of the high plateau of **Plasa.** This road, unfortunately, was built for the illegal exploitation of the rich forests on this side of the mountain. Uncontrolled logging in this part of the country is a major environmental concern. Once on Plasa there is a tiny hut used by hikers and hunters. The culture with these tiny improvised huts is that you are free to enter and sleep if there is no-one else there but you are expected to clean and leave the hut as you found it. Leftover food like sugar, tea or conserves should be left behind for the next guest. The hike across Plasa leads to high peaks around **Velinac** (2,118m) and **Strmac**, with **Diva grabovica** (200m) deep in the valley below. The view on to Pestibrdo is an inspiring one and you may find yourself sitting there for a while just contemplating

Diva grabovica is one of the many hidden wonders of the central Alps of Herzegovina. There are more stunning hikes to be had in this area of the country than anywhere else in the wider region. A guide is advisable as many trails can be overgrown or poorly marked. From Diva the most popular and attractive hike is towards Žljeb and Tise. About an hour and a half's trek up towards Hajdučka vrata is **Žljeb**. The mountain hut here was damaged during the war but still provides primitive shelter if you'd like to camp out. In the dense beech forests above Žljeb is the **Tise** hunting lodge, built for King Karađorđević during the time of the Kingdom of Serbs, Croats and Slovenes. The king trekked up the mountain by horse and this was apparently his favorite hunting spot. Tito also came to Diva grabovica when it was a hunting preserve teeming with mouffons, chamois, bears and wolves. The war took a heavy toll on the wildlife here and it is no longer a legal hunting zone. The long silences in the valley are broken by the squawks of eagles and falcons that nest in the cliffs.

Another great trek from Diva heads towards the mighty rock faces at the end of the valley. After a solid two-hour hike you'll find the largest rock face on the Balkan Peninsula. **Veliki kuk** dominates the skyline with over 1,000m of pure rock. It is climbable but few have done it. A guide and good safety gear is recommended. There are shorter routes marked for novice or average climbers that are challenging and fun. The small shelter, called **Bivak**, was built by a climbing club in Sarajevo and comfortably sleeps six. On the ridge below Veliki kuk is a small picnic area with a magnificent view of neighboring Prenj Mountain. A new cable, called 'silo' in the local language, has been built into the face for some exciting free climbing to the left of the face. Use great caution if you choose to do it solo.

In the village of Diva Grabovica itself, divided by a small ridge, one can find 100% natural organic honey produced by the local villagers. A one-liter jar costs 10 KM. The underwater aquifer systems surface in the first valley where one of the villagers has made a natural fish farm. Several hundred meters after the spot where cold mountain water reaches sunlight is the **Braco and Seka** fish restaurant (no phone). Fresh trout is served and you get to pick the one you want. The restaurant also serves grilled lamb and goat. If you're just looking for a cool drink and a place to sit and admire the scenery: that's possible too.

The footpaths that circle around the village are well maintained, both by goats and their keepers, and are ideal for an easy stroll or a walk with small children. The valley of Diva grabovica is safe from mines. The closest mines to this area are a good four or five-hour hike straight up the mountain.

The highest peak on Čvrsnica, and indeed the highest peak in Herzegovina is Pločna. This peak is a military installation and is off limits to hikers. However, Čvrsnica doesn't only encompass the Neretva Valley side – to the north in **Blidinje Nature Park** is another amazing valley with many more fabulous hiking trails, ski lifts and accommodation. Access is easiest via Tomislav-grad to the northwest but is also possible via the Jablanica – Doljani road. The park is open all year round and the hotel in the valley near Risovac can offer information about hiking and skiing in the region.

Čabulja Mountain

The settlement of Drežnica sits humbly under the massive rock faces of **Čabulja and Čvrsnica Mountains**. Only 20km north of Mostar, it is easily accessed just off the M-17 towards Sarajevo. The **River Drežanka** cuts through the deep valley and 12 canyons feed the Drežanka along its 18km of stunning terrain. It is an ideal car ride for the picturesque views and awe-inspiring canyons. The deeper you travel into the canyon, the further back in time you feel you've gone. The tiny villages that dot the mountainside are remnants of olđworld Europe and a traditional way of life.

With the exception of the **Merkur Hotel** and the **Vrt ciklama** climbing area there is no 'tourism' per se in Drežnica. This guarantees you at the very least an authentic experience not seen even by most Bosnians and Herzegovinians. It is one of those off-the-beaten-track places that have been made accessible by recent road building but no-one other than the locals seem quite aware of it yet. Merkur Hotel (tel: 036 586 052) is situated at the beginning of the canyon where the Drežanka flows into the Neretva River. It has a beautiful bašta (garden) for a meal or just a cool drink. The hotel is a new structure and the service and rooms are modern.

There are hiking trails throughout the canyon but very few are marked. Solo hiking is not recommended in this area as the terrain is harsh and there is the risk of falling rocks. Much of the canyon is loose limestone that can pose hazards to unfamiliar hikers.

Due to the difficult post-war economic situation little attention has been paid to Bosnia and Herzegovina's natural wonders. Prior to the war, most parks and conservation areas offered pre-arranged guided walks but now that service is for the most part non-existent. There are, however, a few eco-tourism operators that provide professional, guided tours in these areas. Scorpio Extreme Sports Club (061 608 130; clubscorpio2004@yahoo.com) from Zenica also offers climbing camps in the region and provides guides and equipment.

PROZOR AND RAMSKO LAKE

Prozor and Ramsko Lake are the northernmost points in Herzegovina. Both Catholics and Muslims inhabit this area. Ramsko Lake is home to Sit Island where the **House of Peace** at the **Franciscan monastery Rama-Ščit** welcomes guests who are looking for peace and quiet, a bit of counseling or just a day of fishing on the lake (tel: 036 780 740; fax: 036 780 680; email: teledom.rama@tel.net.ba; web: www.rama.co.ba). It is run by the Franciscan monks who live there year round. In this monastery, the partisans prepared themselves for their counter-offensive in the Second World War's Battle of the Neretva.

The area is lush and green and offers great fishing, boating, walking and hiking and an interesting look at village life in the surrounding hills. If

Podveležje plateau still maintains its traditional way of life

summer months bring long dry spells
ome highland areas

Sheep shearing festival on
Podveležje plateau

Farmer from Nevesinje

Remnants of an old watermill
near the Zalomka River

Medieval tombstone (stećak) on
the east side of Mt. Velež

you want peace and quiet, look no further - Ramsko Lake will meet your needs. There isn't a 'tourist offer' to speak of but foreign guests are not uncommon, particularly at the monastery. The local villagers are very kind and getting off into the hills you'll find fascinating Catholic villages where women still dress in traditional attire and practice the ancient ritual of tat-tooing crosses on their hands, arms and even foreheads.

Prozor to the east of Ramsko Lake is a small mountain town with not much more to do than walk around and check out life in a small town. The Muslim population, expelled during the war, has returned in large numbers bringing the town back to life a bit. **Motel Rama** in the center of town has a capacity of about 40 with a large restaurant (Splitska ulica bb; tel: 036 771 443; fax 036 771 442; email: info@motel-rama.com; web: www.motel-rama.com). Rates are low at 35 KM per night or 55 KM for a double room. Prozor is a good location if you want to be in between the lake and Blidinje Nature Park. Some of the Muslim villages around Prozor are as fascinating as the Catholic ones.

Just down the road from Prozor is the village of **Duge,** meaning Rain-bow. Duge is blessed with an immense water supply and a powerful water-fall called **Duge Falls.** It is called Rainbow because as the water plummets over 30m to the rocks below the mist mixes with the rays of the sun and almost always creates a rainbow. The locals are fighting a local business-man who wants to build a small dam near the waterfall that would not only ruin the falls, but also the entire ambience of the village.

There is a small fish farm here owned by an old gentleman named Semso. He'll gladly show you the 300-year-old water mills where Tito once hid, and the hidden waterfall located on the upper side of his property. They serve lunch there and it is 100% natural and organic. Plan on staying a while, the food just keeps coming. The trout is wonderful!

A walk through the village is interesting as well. If you have a vehicle and a decent map look for the villages of **Ščipe, Kute** and **Here.** Ščipe is the most distant but attractively situated in the magical highlands between **Bitovnja** and **Vranica Mountains**. The locals are very friendly and the hilly terrain above the village is great for walking, mushroom-picking and finding countless medicinal herbs.

ECO-TOURISM IN HERZEGOVINA

Herzegovina, as well as being a bastion of cultural heritage, pre-serves one of the most beautiful and unique eco-systems in all of Europe. It is here that the Mediterranean and Alpine climates clash, creating conditions for dozens of types of endemic flora and fauna. The mountains are the Dinaric extension of the Swiss Alps and dominate most of Herzegovina's territory. This section will address some of types of birds, fish, animals and herbs found in throughout the region. For the tourist, there are plenty of ways to enjoy the great taste of nature: hiking, biking, fishing, canoe-ing, rafting, bird watching and herb picking are all extremely in-teresting in this area. One can find eco-tourism groups or tour operators for fishing, hiking (see Green Visions), rafting (see Konjic) and canoeing (see Trebižat near Čapljina) in many places. Bird watching can be arranged in Hutovo blato by the park man-agement.

GREEN VISIONS

Green Visions is the country's leading eco-tourism and environmental group based out of Sarajevo. Much of their activities are focused on the central Dinaric Alps which dominate most of central Herzegovina. This company has pioneered the responsible tourism movement in the country and is dedicated to promoting and preserving the natural and cultural heritage of the highland areas. Green Visions has an international team that speaks Bosnian, English, Dutch, Ukranian, and French and has a great corps of seasoned guides. Their philososphy of conscientious tourism honours the leave no trace policy and is committed to 'sharing the wealth' with the struggling highlanders. They are active in lobbying for environmental protection of both the people and the land and work on alternative means of sustainable development for Bosnia and Herzegovina's rural population.

Green Visions specializes in mountain walks and hikes ranging from a nice day trip to a ten day tour of the most amazing terrain in southeast Europe. Accommodation is usually in the homes of the villagers or in mountain huts in the highland regions. Meals are the traditional, organic foods from the highlanders themselves. If you're looking for something authentic...something off the beaten track....something that will make a contribution to the communities you visit....an organic experience with the earth in mind...Green Visions can offer that!

Green Visions offers the following activities:

- Mountain walking and trekking
- Mountain biking
- Rafting
- Village tourism
- Tour skiing
- Cultural heritage tours (rural focus)

Green Visions: Radnička bb, Sarajevo 71000.
Tel/fax: +387 33 717 290;
email: sarajevo@greenvisions.ba;
web: www.greenvisions.ba .

The following section focuses on the Mt. Velež region to the east of Mostar but much of the information applies to the other major mountain regions as well, including: Prenj, Čvrsnica, Čabulja, and Crvanj Mountains in central Herzegovina.

MT. VELEŽ REGION – Blagaj, Nevesinje, and Podveležje

This section was researched and written by *John Snyder*, a team member of the Japan International Cooperation Agency (JICA), who conducted a comprehensive study of the eco-tourism development opportunities in two study areas in Bosnia and Herzegovina. The Mt. Velež region is one of those study areas and the information offered here is a result of extensive research. I'm sure you'll find this small corner of Herzegovina a fascinating part of your experience. For more information on the region check out www.veleztourism.ba.

Location

The Mount Velež Region is located in the south-central part of the Herzegovina region of Bosnia and Herzegovina. The three largest communities in the Mount Velež Region are Blagaj, which is located near the source of the Buna River; Nevesinje, which is located in a secluded mountain valley; and Podveležje which is situated below the summit of Mount Velež. Blagaj has a fascinating history and offers a variety of authentic cultural experiences. Nevesinje is surrounded by wide river valleys and high mountains that offer a diversity of quality outdoor recreation activities and attractions. The village of Podveležje provides access to a remarkable collection of high mountain recreation experiences and spectacular vistas. The entire region is a rich agricultural area that not only grows delicious fruits and vegetables, but also highly sought herbs and aromatic plants.

Climate and weather conditions

Diversity accurately characterizes the climate and weather conditions of the Mount Velež Region. The dramatically different land forms that are located in this region and the influence of its major rivers are responsible for the variable weather conditions that one experiences. The sharply contrasting topography includes large, wide valleys at low elevations such as those located along the Neretva River near Blagaj; the wide valley around Nevesinje that is surrounded by the dramatically fortress-like ramparts of the Velež Mountains; and finally, the tall mountain range of the Velež Mountains dictates the climate of Podveležje. The elevation at Blagaj is only 92 meters, the community of Nevesinje is located at a height of 896 meters, and the highest peak in the Velež Mountains rises to 1,958 meters. The entire region is punctuated with major rivers that flow both above and below the ground. The naturally cold temperatures of the region's rivers and their rapid flow contribute to the rapid movement of airflow in some areas and to dramatic differences in temperatures throughout this region. Logically, the communities of Blagaj, Nevesinje, and Podveležje face distinctly different weather conditions.

The Blagaj area experiences Mediterranean weather conditions. The climate in the Mostar – Blagaj region is generally characterized by mild winters and very hot summers. Fortunately for the residents and visitors of Blagaj, the Buna River provides cool breezes in the summer that result in very comfortable weather conditions.

The Nevesinje area is under the influence of both the Central European climate from the north and Mediterranean climate from the south. The varied relief produces a variety of weather conditions in the vicinity of Nevesinje. Pleasantly cool summers and cold winters are typical for this region. The coldest month of the year is January with an average temperature of –2 degrees C and the hottest months are July and August with an average temperature of 18°C. Autumn is hotter than spring, because of the strong temperature influences of the Adriatic Sea.

The mountain community of Podveležje experiences very comfortable summers but also the most severe winters in the Mount Velež Region. Many persons from the Mostar region go to the Podveležje region in the summer to escape the heat of the low valleys. The Podveležje weather conditions are also characterized by strong wind. The visitor will quickly learn that the lack of trees which permit many beautiful views also contributes to a windy experience. There is no forest to shelter a person from the wind. Persons pursuing outdoor recreation activities in this area are advised to be well prepared for these windy conditions. Wearing or carrying warm clothing, gloves, and a hat is advisable for a comfortable experience.

Temperature

The Mount Velež Region belongs to a Sub-Mediterranean climate zone that features a long and warm summer season with high temperatures during the day. The temperatures between Blagaj, Nevesinje, and Podveležje are quite different. Information from weather stations located at Blagaj and Nevesinje illustrate the sharp temperature contrasts that exist in the Mount Velež Region. The coldest monthly average temperature in Nevesinje is -2°C, and the warmest monthly average temperature is 18°C. In contrast, the coldest monthly average temperature in Blagaj is 4.8°C, and the warmest monthly average temperature is 24.7°C

Monthly average temperature in the Mount Velež Region

Unit: °C

Station	Jan.	Feb.	Mar.	Apr.	May	Jun.	Jul.	Aug.	Sep.	Oct.	Nov.	Dec.
Nevesinje[1]	-2	0	2	8	12	14	18	18	14	8	4	0
Blagaj[2]	4.8	6.6	9.6	13.3	17.9	21.5	24.7	24.2	20.4	15.3	10.1	6.2

Source: 1) Institute for Urbanism, BiH; 2) State Hydro Meteorological Institute, Mostar

Precipitation

Annual average precipitation in Nevesinje and Blagaj is more than 1,500mm. This average exceeds the annual average precipitation of the country. There is, however, a dry season and this lasts from June to August.

Monthly Average Precipitation in the Mount Velež Region

Unit: mm

Station	Jan.	Feb.	Mar.	Apr.	May	Jun.	Jul.	Aug.	Sep.	Oct.	Nov.	Dec.
Nevesinje[1]	200	200	150	125	100	80	60	50	150	200	200	200
Blagaj[2]	165	148	150	127	102	78	43	76	96	151	200	179

Source: 1) Institute for Urbanism, BiH; 2) State Hydro Meteorological Institute, Mostar

FISHING

Introduction

Several quality sport fishing opportunities are available in the rivers and lakes located throughout the Mount Velež Region. Each community in this region can provide uniquely different fishing experiences. These waters provide superb habitat for a diversity of large and healthy fish species. The sports angler can employ either leisurely or very active fishing techniques. The rivers can be fished by the streamside angler using spin casting gear or by the angler who wades the currents with fly fishing tackle. More leisurely approaches are readily available by means of boat fishing in the lakes.

The information contained in this guide provides the prospective angler with descriptions of the rivers and lakes; the types of fish that inhabit these waters; advice regarding licenses and permits; and contact information for sport fishing clubs that are well qualified to provide fish guiding and other support services.

Fishing areas

THE RIVERS

The rivers of the Mount Velež Region are fascinating because they appear as rushing torrents or smooth rolling streams and then disappear underground only to re-appear at another location in the region. The enormous and complex geological karst formations contain underground passages that allow the rivers to travel both above and below the ground. Most remarkably, these rivers do in fact travel under the Velež Mountains. Seasonal differences can be equally dramatic. A river may fill a valley in the spring with water and then sink below the surface during the end of the summer for lack of sufficient flow. When the water flows underground the purity of the water is enhanced and its temeperature gets quite cold. This creates very special conditions needed for quality fishing.

There are three major rivers located in the Mount Velež Region and a variety of smaller tributaries. Each of these rivers and streams has unique water conditions and fishing characteristics. The names of the three major rivers are the Zalomka, the Buna, and the Bunica.

The Zalomka River

The biggest and the most important river in the Nevesinje valley is the Zalomka River. This large river traces huge curves as it flows northwards through the entire valley. In some locations it is very prominent and wide and in other locations quite narrow. The amount of water in each section of the river can vary considerably by both location and season of the year. Its annual average rate of flow has been estimated to be 300 m3/sec. The season of the year will impact the flow of water significantly. During the springtime, when the snow runs off the mountains, the river can rise dramatically. The snows, when increased by the spring rains, can produce a substantial surge of flowing water. In the summer season the Zalomka's water flow decreases significantly.

The following types of fish and crabs can be found in the Zalomka River: California (Rainbow) Trout, Brown Trout, Rockery Crab, Puddle crab. A brief description and illustrations of these species are provided in this guide.

The Sports Fishing Club (SFC) "Zalomka" controls fishing access to sections of the Zalomka River. This ownership is important to insure both excellent management of the fishery and a quality fishing recreation experience. The best river fishing occurs along two sections of the Zalomka River located south of the town of Nevesinje. The first sport fishing section of the Zalomka River, located directly south of the town, flows from west to east and is approximately 10 km in length. The second section of the river is located north east of town and flows in a meandering pattern. Its flow begins in southeast direction and then bends towards the northeast. Both of these locations are easily accessible by vehicle and the visitor will enjoy the beautiful vistas that surround these sites.

The Buna River

One of the major rivers in the Mount Velež Region is the Buna River that flows through the center of the community of Blagaj. The Buna River has many unique characteristics. The source of the Buna is one of Europe's largest natural springs. Measurements of this natural spring indicates that water is flowing out of the ground at the rate of 36m3/s. From this remarkable water source, the Buna flows towards the west for a distance of approximately 6 km to the Neretva River.

The flow of the Buna River water is also believed to be an important source of water for the Zalomka River. Investigations of the underground water channels indicate that the Buna contributes water to the Zalomka River system. One channel of the Buna

River literally sinks underground in the vicinity of Ponor and then re-appears in the Zalomka River system. The underground route of the Buna river system has been explored by French cave diving teams. The result of this unique water distribution system is that the Buna River provides an important source of water to the communities of Blagaj, Nevesinje, and Mostar.

The constant cold temperature of the Buna River makes it an ideal habitat for trout. An abundance of California (Rainbow) trout may be found in this river. Fishing in the Buna River is allowed from the western boundary of the Town of Blagaj to the Neretva River. From its natural source to the western boundary of the Town of Blagaj fishing is prohibited. Given its nearly ideal, constant temperature and purity, the Buna River is also the site of a trout fish hatchery run by Norfish. The angler who, for whatever reason, is unable to catch a trout will not go hungry. The angler may be assured that the Norfish Restaurant will be pleased to serve a splendid trout dinner.

The Bunica River

The Bunica River is a tributary to the Buna River. The source of the Bunica River is 4 km away from the community of Blagaj. The Bunica River begins in the village Malo Polje. At the mouth of the Bunica River, where it enters the Buna River, there is a sport–recreation center called "Bunica". People are attracted to this location because there is evidence that the Bunica water is especially healthy and can provide therapeutic help to people. Given the purity of this water, its remoteness and sport fishing opportunities, this river is a potentially excellent recreation location. Unfortunately, however, the banks and shoreline of this river were the location of intense conflict during the war and the continued presence of land mines remains a very real danger. Recreation activity in this region should only be pursued with a knowledgeable guide.

THE LAKES

The Nevesinje region has many large and small lakes. The small lakes are natural and these are located in the upper elevations of the mountains that surround the Nevesinje Valley. By example, there is an especially attractive mountain lake located approximately 4 km east of the Velež Mountain Range. Naturally occurring lakes along the floor of the valley have seasonal characteristics. In the winter and spring they are generally full, but by the middle to the end of summer they can be nearly dry.

The largest lake in Nevesinje Valley is a man made lake called Lake Alagovac. It is located at the foot of the Velež Mountains and its water surface area covers approximately 40 ha. Lake Alagovac is located approximately 4 km north of the Town of Nevesinje and can be easily accessed by road. This lake is the source of the town's water supply. The water quality of the lake is excellent and the town carefully manages the water resources to sustain water quality.

Trophy fishing is available at Lake Alagovac. The trophy species include White Amur and Pike. The Sportfishing opportunities also include Dace, Carp, Lake Trout, and Catfish. A complete description and illustrations of these species are provided in this guide.

Streamside and boat fishing are allowed in Lake Alagovac. The only prohibited region is in the vicinity of the town's water supply facilities. The fishery at Lake Alagovac is managed by the local fishing club, SFC "Zalomka" Nevesinje. The club provides fishing information, guides, and support services such as transportation.

Types of fish

White Amur (Ctenopharyngondon idella Val.)

Authorized Fishing Association	"Zalomka" Nevesinje
Fishing License (Daily)	domestic - 10 KM
	tourist - 30 KM
Location	Lake Alagovac
Max. Allowed Daily Catch	4 pieces
Min. Allowed Length Catch	60 cm
Closed Season	01 April - 31 May
Allowed Equipment	Two rods with two fish-hooks
Allowed Baits	All natural and artifical baits except alive baits

Carp (Cuprinus caprio L.)

Authorized Fishing Association	"Zalomka" Nevesinje
Fishing License (Daily)	domestic - 10 KM
	tourist - 30 KM
Location	Lake Alagovac
Max. Allowed Daily Catch	4 pieces
Min. Allowed Length Catch	30 cm
Closed Season	01 April - 31 May
Allowed Equipment	Two rods with two fish-hooks
Allowed Baits	All natural and artificial baits except alive baits

Pike - Perch (Stizostedion Luciperka L.)

Authorized Fishing Association	"Zalomka" Nevesinje
Fishing License (Daily)	domestic - 10 KM
	tourist - 30 KM
Location	Lake Alagovac
Max. Allowed Daily Catch	4 pieces
Min. Allowed Length Catch	40 cm
Closed Season	01 March - 31 May
Allowed Equipment	Two rods with two fish-hooks
Allowed Baits	All natural and artificial baits except alive baits

Tolstolobik (Hipophtalmichthys molitrx Val.)

Authorized Fishing Association	"Zalomka" Nevesinje
Fishing License (Daily)	domestic - 10 KM
	tourist - 30 KM
Location	Lake Alagovac
Max. Allowed Daily Catch	4 pieces
Min. Allowed Length Catch	60 cm
Closed Season	01 March - 31 May
Allowed Equipment	Two rods with two fish-hooks
Allowed Baits	All natural and artificial baits except alive baits

Catfish (Silurus glanis L.)

Authorized Fishing Association	"Zalomka" Nevesinje
Fishing License (Daily)	domestic - 10 KM
	tourist - 30 KM
Location	Lake Alagovac
Max. Allowed Daily Catch	4 pieces
Min. Allowed Length Catch	60 cm
Closed Season	16 April - 15 June
Allowed Equipment	Two rods with two fish-hooks
Allowed Baits	All natural and artifical baits except alive baits

Dace (Leuciscus tursyi Hecak)

Authorized Fishing Association	"Zalomka" Nevesinje
Fishing License (Daily)	domestic - 10 KM
	tourist - 30 KM
Location	Lake Alagovac
Max. Allowed Daily Catch	4 pieces
Min. Allowed Length Catch	20 cm
Closed Season	16 April - 15 June
Allowed Equipment	Two rods with two fish-hooks
Allowed Baits	All natural and artifical baits except alive baits

California Trout (Salmo gairdneri R , Salmo irideus G.)

Authorized Fishing Association	"Zalomka" Nevesinje
Fishing License (Daily)	domestic - 10 KM
	tourist - 30 KM
Location	River Zalomka
	River Batuša
	River Buna
Max. Allowed Daily Catch	5 pieces
Min. Allowed Length Catch	25 cm
Closed Season	-
Allowed Equipment	Two rods with two fish-hooks
Allowed Baits	All natural and artificial baits except alive baits

Brown Trout (Salmo trutta m. Fario L.)

Authorized Fishing Association	"Zalomka" Nevesinje
Fishing License (Daily)	domestic - 10 KM
	tourist - 30 KM
Location	River Zalomka
	River Batuša
	River Buna
Max. Allowed Daily Catch	5 pieces
Min. Allowed Length Catch	25 cm
Closed Season	-
Allowed Equipment	Two rods with two fish-hooks
Allowed Baits	All natural and artificial baits except alive baits

Rockery Crab (Astacus terrentium Schr.)

Authorized Fishing Association	"Zalomka" Nevesinje
Fishing License (Daily)	domestic - 10 KM
	tourist - 30 KM
Location	River Zalomka
Max. Allowed Daily Catch	-
Min. Allowed Length Catch	8 cm
Close Time	01 November - 15 May
Allowed Equipment	Two rods with two fish - hooks
Allowed Baits	All natural and artificial baits except alive baits

Puddle Crab (Astacus leptodaetybus Esch.)

Authorized Fishing Association	"Zalomka" Nevesinje
Fishing License (Daily)	domestic - 10 KM
	tourist - 30 KM
Location	River Zalomka
Max. Allowed Daily Catch	-
Min. Allowed Length Catch	8 cm
Close Time	01 November - 15 May
Allowed Equipment	Two rods with two fish-hooks
Allowed Baits	All natural and artificial baits except alive baits

Sport fishing regulations

Fishing in the Mount Velež Region is managed by two fishing clubs. One of the clubs is called Sports Fishing Club "Zalomka" and it is headquartered in Nevesinje. The second club is called The Fish Association and it is located in Blagaj. These clubs have played a very important role in sustaining both the fish population and the water quality in the region. As a result of their responsible management both the resident and non-resident angler can enjoy a high quality recreation experience.

Sports Fishing Club "Zalomka" Nevesinje

Fishing in the rivers and lakes near the Town of Nevesinje is managed by the Sports Fishing Club "Zalomka" Nevesinje. Specific fishing locations managed by the club include Lake Alagovac, the River Zalomka from the bridge called Kunjak to its drainage in the Neretva River, and the Batuša River.

There are three fishing seasons in the Nevesinje region. The first is a spring season that begins in March and extends through mid-April. The second begins in June and continues until the arrival of winter weather in either November or December. The trout fishing season lasts from March through October.

The sports fishing club performs several management functions to sustain the fish stocks in Lake Alagovac and the Zalomka River. They regularly stock these waters and they organize fish–keeping services in order to protect fish reserves. A vital part of the club's management functions include protecting water quality. The success of these efforts is evident in the size of the fish. By example, Amur over 50 kilos, Smooch at 10 kilos, and Catfish at 50 kilos can be caught in the fishery.

Licences

The daily Fishing Licence cost is 10 KM per day for residents and 30 KM for foreign tourists. A daily licence is available from 5 a.m. to 10 p.m.

Guides and fishing equipment

Sports Fishing Club "Zalomka" has trained guides. Six members of the Fishing Club serve as guides. These people have many years of experience and are well acquainted with the region's fishing conditions.

The most popular fishing equipment used in the Nevesinje Region are spinning rods and reels. The spinning rods are usually a two piece sectional rod that is 3.5 meters (10 feet) in length. The strength of the rods should provide 15 to 40 grams of action. All types of spinning reels are appropriate for these fishing conditions. Spinning reels may be of either open or closed face design.

Numerous patterns and styles of lures and artificial bait are effective in the Nevesinje and Blagaj lakes and streams. The Rapala type lures are especially effective, as well as Heddon lures. In regards to specific lure colors, size, and action and artificial bait patterns, the guides will provide advice to the angler. As always, the type of fish, season, and lake and river conditions will dictate the appropriate type of lure.

A limited amount of fly fishing currently occurs in the Nevesinje Valley, but the Zalomka River offers prime conditions for trophy trout fishing. Suggested fly fishing equipment would include fly rods of 4, 5, and 6 weights for streams and rivers, and high mountain lakes. Rod weights of 7, 8, and 9 would be appropriate for Lake Alagovac. The heavier weights would be essential to cope with strong winds that can occur in the region.

The sport fishing club can arrange vehicles for transport, but does not rent fishing equipment and tackle. Although they are not currently able to rent fishing equipment, they do allow guests to borrow their members' equipment.

Contacts

Nevesinje Youth Initiative; tel/fax: 059 610 120;

omladina@teol.net

Contact person - Mr. Milan Damjanac, phone number 059 / 601 – 790

The Sports Fishing Club "Zalomka" has a website and uses this to respond to inquiries and book fishing trips.

Green Visions tel/fax: 033 717 290.

Fishing Association - Blagaj

A new but very active fishing club has been established in Blagaj. The name of this club is Fishing Association – Blagaj. This fishing association is currently in the process of registering their association with the appropriate government agencies. There are 90 members and two fish–keepers in this association.

The association manages three rivers in the Blagaj area. Those rivers include the Buna, the Bunica, and a small section of the Neretva Rivers. From the source of the Buna River to Karađoz-beg bridge fishing is forbidden. From the Karađoz-beg bridge to Lehin bridge fishing is allowed for daily licence users. From Lehin bridge to the Sports Recreation Center called "Bunica" fishing is allowed with daily and monthly licenses.

The rivers in the Blagaj region provide quality habitat for California Trout, Brook Trout, Brown Trout, Dentex, Chub, and various types of crabs. The trout species spawn in the fall. The allowable catch is 4 fish per day.

The fishing season begins on May 1 and lasts until October 31. Most importantly, fishing is only allowed on specific days of the week. The fishing days are Wednesday, Saturday, Sunday, and holidays. The limited number of fishing days helps sustain the fishery and reduces the potentially negative impact of the 4 fish per day allowable catch.

Licences

A daily fishing license costs 50 KM for foreign tourists.

Guides and fishing equipment

The angler is limited to a few types of lures, baits, and artificial baits. Only one type of bait is permitted as well as one type of small fly and a type of butterfly. The Fishing Association will provide information to anglers regarding the types of tackle that may be used.

The most popular types of fishing equipment used in the Blagaj Region are spinning rods and reels. The spinning rods are usually a two piece sectional rod that is 3 and half meters (10 feet) in length. The strength of the rods should provide 15 to 40 grams of action. All types of spinning reels are appropriate for these fishing conditions. Spinning reels may be of either open or closed face design. Members of the Fishing Association will rent fishing equipment to tourist anglers.

Contacts

Association of Sports Fishermen - Mustafa Batlak, president; Tel: 036 572 166

Green Visions based out of Sarajevo also organizes tours to the region – including fishing, hiking, climbing and village tourism.

Astra Travel is a locally based travel agency that can make arrangements for fishing, accommodation, and transport.

MOUNTAINEERING AND TECHNICAL CLIMBING

The Velež Mountain Range offers a variety of challenging climbing and mountaineering experiences. Mount Velež is the summit of this range and this mountain is 1,958 meters above sea level. The ascent distance from the valley floor in Blagaj to the summit is nearly 1,900 meters.

The headwalls along the eastern face of Velež Mountains

The most challenging technical climbs in the Velež Mountains are located along the headwalls of the eastern face of the mountain range. These walls have extremely steep pitches and require expert technical mountaineering skills. The difficulty of these climbs is evidenced by the fact that mountaineers attempting an assault upon Mt. Everest practice in this region. These are rock ramparts and few ascent routes have been explored. For the climber seeking remoteness and solitude from the crowds this is a great place to climb.

Easier routes to the summit

The north and south flanks of the Velež Mountains offer rigorous climbing experiences that require basic mountaineering skills. Access to these routes can be time consuming, but the scenery along the routes and locations for camps will compensate the climber who chooses one of these routes.

The western side of the Velež Mountains is definitely the easiest route to the summit and requires minimal mountaineering skills and equipment. Good hiking boots and warm clothing define the essential equipment requirements for this route. The western side of Mount Velež is a relatively gentle sloping, treeless moraine. Views of the Buna River and Neretva River valleys may be seen continuously during this mountaineering experience.

Land mines

Great caution is required for all backcountry activities in the Mount Velež region because of the continued presence of minefields in certain areas. Unfortunately, the easiest route to the summit along the western face has the largest number of mines. Most importantly, Nevesinje does NOT have land mines and therefore the eastern side of the Velež Mountain Range offers considerably safer mountaineering and hiking experiences. ANY of these routes should be used ONLY with the assistance of an experienced mountain guide.

Mountain associations

Bosnia and Herzegovina has three major mountaineering organizations located throughout the country. Each of the three major organizations has several clubs associated with them. This network of mountain clubs is very important because they provide the guides and any emergency search and rescue operations that may be required. There are two mountaineering clubs in the Mostar / Mount Velež Region and the community of Nevesinje is in the process of creating a club. All of these clubs are supported by the Klub Spasavalaca 2000 Rescue Club, Sarajevo which is capable of providing technical climbing support and conducting difficult mountain rescue operations.

Prenj Mountain Association

Persons seeking technical/expert guide services for the Velež Mountain Region should contact the Prenj Mountain Association. This club is based in Mostar and has perhaps 200 members. In addition, they own 3 camp sites in the Velež Mountain area. The only one remaining in operation is in the Rujište area, north of Mt. Velež. The Prenj Mountain Association also has close relationships with several mountaineering clubs in both Bosnia and Croatia.

Mountaineering services in Podveležje

At an elevation of 720 m above sea-level at the foot of Mount Velež, the small community of Podveležje provides an excellent base from which to pursue mountaineering activities. This community consists of a 13 high mountain villages spread across an area of 160 km². The people living in these villages continue a long tradition of livestock grazing. The climate in this region is especially attractive in the summer.

The Podveležje area has great conditions for climbing and mountaineering. Although there is no mountaineering association, the farmers from Podveležje are very skillful climbers and have expert knowledge of the mountains. Very capable persons from this community have created two hiking routes to the summit and these people can provide guide services that will enable tourists reach the summit of Mount Velež. In addition, at the foot of Mount Velež there are two huts with 10 beds which can be used as quarters for the night.

Motel Sunce - Contact person: Ismet Stranjak, Podveležje bb; tel: 036/560-082 / 061/467-644

Green Visions based out of Sarajevo organizes hiking and mountaineering trips to this region and has experienced and professional guides.

Mountaineering in Nevesinje

The mountaineering and climbing conditions in the vicinity of Nevesinje are excellent. The visitor may select either leisurely or strenuous mountaineering experiences. The Velež Mountains may be approached from several, well established hiking trails located on the eastern, southern, and northern sides of the mountains. Many of these routes offer leisurely hiking experiences. Access to these hiking routes is excellent. There are forest roads that provide direct access to the trailheads (starting points). In additon, there are two mountain huts that can be used for overnight stays by mountaineers and others using the backcountry. One of the huts can be visited by a car because there is direct road access from the Village of Sopilja.

One of the most attractive locations for mountaineering in the Nevesinje region is in the vicinity of Mount Crvanj. This area has excellent and very scenic paths to the summit of the mountains. On the route to Mount Crvanj there is a very beautiful lake. A mountain hut near this lake is currently being renovated. All of these natural and man made features will provide enjoyable recreation experiences for persons visiting the Crvanj mountain region.

Again, the technical climbing challenges of the Velež Mount begin when the mountaineer reaches the immense headwalls of those mountains. The rock walls, snow and ice, and weather conditons contribute to the difficulty of this climb. As stated earlier, skilled guiding and proper equipment are required to attempt these technical climbs. The Prenj Mountain Club or the Klub Spasavalaca 2000 Rescue Club and Green Visions can provide this type of support services.

WILDLIFE AND BIRDING

The Herzegovina wildlife experiences are unique to Europe. By example, Bosnia and Herzegovina provides a critical habitat for thriving populations of European Brown Bear, Chamois, Wolves, Wild Boar, Wild Cat (Lynx and Bobcat), and River Otter. These species are virtually extinct in the rest of Europe. The abundance of wildlife results from the enormous expanses of wilderness that still exist in the mountainous terrain of this region. The wilderness is further endowed with an abundance of water that provides a rich habitat for a remarkable diversity of wildlife. The geography of the Balkans also plays a vital role in sustaining wildlife, especially birds. Herzegovina and the southern Balkans represent the shortest migratory bird route between central Europe and Africa. The unique wilderness setting offers both a sanctuary for the animals and also a challenge to viewing them safely. The tourist may pursue wildlife viewing and nature photography by means of nature hikes, guided tours, and photo safaris. For wildlife photographers, it is valuable to know that the excellent air quality and abundant sunshine throughout the Herzegovina region provides excellent conditions for capturing wildlife images.

Herzegovina's geographic location represents an enormous opportunity to enjoy unique birding experiences. The Balkan Peninsula represents one of the world's most significant bird migration paths between the continents of Europe and Africa. Tens of thousands of birds migrate through Herzegovina each spring and fall. A total of 240 bird species have been positively identified in the country. Most of these are migratory, but because of the great abundance of water and cover several resident bird species may also be found in Herzegovina. Based on extensive field observations and research performed by local ornithologists a bird species list for Herzegovina has been produced. This is an important and rewarding location to visit for those persons seeking to add to their bird "life lists".

Photo safari guide services

Guide services for photo safaris are provided by the traditional hunting clubs in the communities of Nevesinje, Podveležje, and Blagaj. The members of these organizations have many years of experience and knowledge regarding the wildlife in the Mount Velež Region.

Hunters' Association"Srndać" Nevesinje, Obilića bb. Nevesinje; tel: 065 547 845

Hunting Club Velež, Podveležje bb 88000 Mostar; tel: 061 371 370

Hunting Club "Golub" Blagaj; tel: 036 572 006

The Scouts Association cooperates with the Golub Club to provide photo safaris. The Scouts were established in 1962 and their organization was renewed again in 2002. The Scouts have visited different places to determine suitability for camping. Photo safaris are organized with their help. The contact person of the Scouts Association Blagaj is Mirsad Studenović.

AGRICULTURAL PRODUCTS AND ATTRACTIONS

Agriculture provides the economic base of The Mount Velež Region. The region produces honey, dairy products, wines, fruits, and a diversity of field crops. For the tourist interested in naturally grown and processed agricultural products, the region has a lot to offer. By example, honey, cheeses, and dairy products are still produced in the traditional ways.

The community of Blagaj is located near the Neretva River Valley which produces a large variety of food products and aromatic crops. The fruits and vegetables are especially delicious. This area is especially famous for the aromatic plants that it grows, especially lavender. The expansive fields of lavender in bloom are a beautiful sight.

Nevesinje is particularly well known for its fruits and berries. The growing conditions in this region are well suited for growing plums, apples, pears, sour cherries, currants, raspberries, and strawberries. Nevesinje frequently enjoys large harvests of these fruits and berries and ships part of this harvest to food processing plants. But the visitor can treat themselves to the homemade fruit products available throughout these valleys. Home production includes jams, juices, and a very high quality brandy.

The diverse species of natural vegetation growing on the Podveležje plateau include a wide variety of herbs that have medicinal and aromatic properties. The local population collects them and subsidizes their incomes by selling them to the herbal processing facilities located in the surrounding area. Guide services are available that will let the visitor experience these plants in the wild. There are literally hundreds of plants that are either edible or have medicinal purposes and the visitor may spend a very pleasurable day viewing, learning, and tasting these valuable plants.

For tourists interested in unique animals, Podveležje has a very distinct breed of horse. The Podveležje Hill Horse is an animal that has been specifically bred for the steep slopes and cold conditions of the region. This horse is a small, tough, and extremely strong animal that plays a vital role in the lives of the nomadic people who graze their livestock in the Velez Mountains. For centuries the Podveležje Hill Horse steadily pulled or carried the essential shelters, equipment and supplies of the Velež Mountain people to their several camps located throughout the mountains. The Podveležje Hill Horse continues to play an important role in this unique nomadic way of life and visitors are encouraged to learn more about both this rare animal and the nomadic way of life it helps to sustain.

Types of herbs and mushrooms and collection calendar for the Mount Velež Region

Forest Products	Collecting Calendar
Wild cherry	June
Wild pear	September – October
Wild apple	October
Cornel	October
Sloe, blackberry	September – October
Hazelnut	October
Bilberry	October

Mushrooms	**Collecting Calendar**
Boletus mushrooms	
Yellow chanterelle	
Button mushroom	Summer and autumn
Bukovača	
Maslenica	
Smrčak	

Medicinal Herbs	**Collecting Calendar**
Linden flower	
Elder flower	
Hawthorn flower	
Blackberry flower	
Klamath flower	
Vervain flower	Collection period: May, June and July
Black thorn flower	
Meadow saffron flower	
Camomile flower	
Mint flower	

Medicinal Herbs	**Collecting Calendar**
Hawthorn	
Dog rose	
Mountain pine	
Bilberry	
Plod mukinje	Collection period: September and October
Raspberry	
Blackberry	
Thorns	
Strawberry	

Medicinal Herbs	**Collecting Calendar**
Gentian root	
Wild tobacco root	Collection period: September and October
Herbs	
Sallow	
Horse-tail	
Wild thyme	Collection period: June - September
Hernia	
Sweet fern	
Nettle	

AGRICULTURAL CONTACTS

Tourists who wish to view these agricultural activities and purchase these products should contact the following organization: "Perfeto" Nevesinje (phone number 059 601723, and 065 628 623).

For persons interested in the local beekeepers and their honey products, tourists are encouraged to contact the Apiarist Association 'Ulište' Blagaj. This organization was created to ensure the quality of the honey production. The contact person Mustafić Meho. The telephone number is 061 203 131.

CAVE EXPLORATION

Unique natural conditions

The environmental conditions in the Mount Velež Region have combined to produce numerous caves and a remarkable underground river system. The types of rocks in this region are predominantly dolomite and limestone and the geological formations in this region are known as karsts. This is the world's largest concentration of this type of geology. The region also has an abundance of both underground water and precipitation. The combination of the water and rock in Herzergovina results in dramatic changes in the landscape. The rock is extremely vulnerable to water erosion and the combination of these natural dynamics resulted in the creation of extraordinarly complex caves and underground streams. The caves and underground rivers are constantly increasing in size as the erosion process continues. To date, the locations of 20 large caves have been identified in the Mount Velež Region. As exploration continues it is certain that more caves will be discovered. The exploraration process involves an amazing combination of both spelunking and scuba skills.

The Blagaj Caves

The most prominent caves in Blagaj are located either in or near the Buna River. The source of the Buna is, in fact, the entry to an enormous cave system. Research and mapping of this cave system has been conducted by a team of French cave experts. They have used underwater scuba diving techniques to explore the caves. Their research indicates that the cave extends into the mountain for a distance of 385 m from the spring. The underground river found in this cave flows 68m below the ground. The cave has numerous decorations called stalactites that hang from the roof of the cave. The caves above the Buna's spring are also the habitat of white-headed vulture. This is a rare species of bird that is a significant attraction for both birders and wildlife photographers.

The Green Cave

During prehistoric time the caves in the Mount Velež Region provided shelter to the people of this region. The most notable example of this is Green Cave where signs of human settlement
from two different Neolithic periods were found. Archaeological
research determined that the oldest artefacts in Green Cave are
rare examples from the Impress culture. These ancient people
lived in the Stolac and Trebinje areas of this region in 6500 BC.
The second ancient group of people lived in the cave between
3000 and 2800 BC. A variety of ceramic products provide evidence of their lives. All of the artefacts are now in the Earth Museum in Sarajevo.

The Nevesinje Caves

The majority of known caves in the Mount Velež Region are located in the vicinity of Nevesinje. A total of 15 caves are located
to the north and south of the Town of Nevesinje. The most famous and attractive cave in this area is called Cave Novakuša. It
contains a multitude of stalagmites and stalactites. These stone
pillars and columns provide beautiful decorations.

The Podveležje Caves

The Podveležje caves provide habitat for a variety of rare birds.
There are many sorts of birds that live in various caves and cavi-
ties located throughout this area. Examples of bird species that
use the caves for their habitat include: rock pigeon, falcon, eagle,
sparrow-hawk, owl, and little owl.

The cave exploration experience

There are two types of caving experiences and each requires expert knowledge and special equipment. Many of the cave systems are actually underground rivers. In order to explore these
caves it is essential to have a very competent knowledge of both
caves and scuba diving techniques. The dry cave requires both
knowledge of caves and technical climbing skills. Organizations
in the Mount Velež Region are interested in providing these specialized types of recreation experiences, but the technical support systems required to accomplish that are not yet in place.

VISITOR SAFETY AND PRECAUTIONS

Terrain and animals

The majority of the terrain in Mount Velež Region is either flat
river valleys or forested hills that can be easily hiked. Some locations in the Velež Mountains, like the Velež Headwalls are, of
course, very steep. Travel in those areas requires substantial tech-

nical climbing skills. The tourist can experience a rapid increase in elevation in this region. For those persons with breathing difficulties or who may have problems acclimating, caution is suggested when traveling from the valleys to the mountains.

Clothing recommendations

Each of the communities in the Mount Velež Region experiences distinctly different weather.

Given the generally warm temperatures, tourists in Blagaj will want clothing that keeps them comfortably cool. There are a variety of sacred Muslim sites in Blagaj, and in respect for the local culture all persons should be conservatively dressed. For most of the year, tourists should be advised to protect themselves from protracted exposure to the sun. A hat and sun block lotion are strongly recommended. Comfortable footwear is appropriate. In contrast with other parts of Mount Velež Region, rugged hiking boots are not needed in the Town of Blagaj.

The perpetually windy conditions of Mount Velež and the community of Podvelež will warrants clothing that is suitable for cool or cold weather. Hats and gloves are also very advisable. Because the weather can change quickly, rain protection is strongly recommended. The wind changes can rapidly change the weather conditions and the tourist needs to be prepared for those changes.

Touring in the vicinity of Nevesinje will require clothing that is appropriate for travel in mountainous areas and in high mountain valleys. Daytime temperatures in the summer are very comfortable, but the night time temperatures are quite a bit lower. The weather moves quickly through this region and rain or snow storms can suddenly occur.

Layering clothing is an effective technique and it is strongly recommended to stay comfortably warm and dry. The "base layer" is the clothing next to your skin and it is important that this layer remain comfortable and as dry as possible throughout the recreation experience. The second, "intermediate layer" provides insulation and the clothing worn in this layer essentially regulates the person's temperature. The third "outer layer" is the shell that protects a person from the elements such as rain, wind, or snow. A good hat is recommended with a brim for keeping both the sun and the water off. In the spring and fall months, gloves are suggested, especially for anglers.

Proper footwear will promote an enjoyable outdoor experience in the vicinity of Podvelež and Nevesinje. The footwear should provide both support and traction. The mountainous terrain has steep slopes that require good traction. A sturdy hiking boot with a lug type sole will provide excellent traction, even during wet conditions.

Wildlife: hazards and safety precautions

The Herzegovina wildlife conditions suggest the need to take some common sense safety precautions. The dominant predators, such as the bears, wolves and wild boar, have no fear of humans and thus must be viewed with extreme caution and with a competent knowledge of their behavior.

Bears: The European brown bear (*Ursus arctos*) inhabits Herzegovina and is especially prevalent in the mountainous areas of the country. Sighting one of these majestic animals can add a lot to a trip. These animals can be safely viewed from elevated structures and from a distance. Contact with bears should be treated with respect and avoided whenever possible. Bears are unpredictable and should never be underestimated. Their sense of smell is extraordinary. Their strength is enormous. And their speed on both land and water is phenomenal. By example, on land bears can travel at 15 m per second and they can easily swim distances of 6 to 8 km.

Confrontations with this animal are rare. Common sense is the best protection available. Make noise while traveling in bear country. They are not seeking a confrontation and noise will alert them to a person presence and they will most probably abandon the area. The two occasions when they will not abandon an area is (1) when there are cubs that require protection, and (2) when they are protecting game – their next meal.

The best advice when encountering a bear is as follows: do not run, as this will trigger their predator instincts and they will quickly pursue and overtake you; back away slowly; if an attack is imminent then lay on then ground and curl into a ball covering your head and neck with your arms; do not approach bear cubs, as the mother is nearby and will defend them from any threat.

The smell of food in the backcountry will attract bears and other predators such as wolves. The transport, storage, cooking, and disposal of food must all be accomplished in such a way as to minimize odors. This includes fish that have been caught. Bears are omnivores. They will eat anything, and their preferred target is the one that requires the least work. Stealing food from a campsite is easier than hunting, so given the choice the bear will invade a campsite or inspect a backpack to obtain food.

Wolves: The wolf (*Cannis lupus*) roams freely throughout Herzegovina. They will avoid humans. If wolves are seen then attempt to stay upwind of their position. Allow them to migrate through your area.

Wild Boar: These animals also roam freely through Herzegovina. Because these animals are aggressively hunted, they fear man. However, these animals are belligerent and are especially dangerous when protecting their young.

Poisonous Snakes

For tourists who wish to hike in Herzegovina it is important to know about the poisonous snakes that inhabit the country and the safety precautions needed to avoid those animals. The information provided below summarizes this information.

Viper, Common Adder

The most common poisonous snake found in Bosnia and Herzegovina is the Viper, Common adder, *Vipera berus*. This snake is widely distributed throughout all of Europe although there is also a subspecies of this snake called the Bosnian Viper, *Vipera berus bosniensis* that inhabits only the Balkan mountains.

Description: This snake has a thick body, a triangular head, with a characteristic V-shaped mark. Its color is variable. Males are normally black while females have been described as "russet red". Both usually carry the characteristic zigzag markings down the back, but some plain black or red individuals occur.

Characteristics: The common adder is a small true viper that has a short temper and often strikes without hesitation. Its venom is hemotoxic, destroying blood cells and causing tissue damage. Most injuries occur to campers, hikers, and field workers. While the poison is not normally dangerous to humans, medical attention should be immediately sought if bitten.

Habitat and distribution: Common adders are found in a variety of habitats, from grassy fields to rocky slopes, and on farms and cultivated lands. They are found from sea level to up to 3,000 m high, in the edges of woods or in clearings, in peat-bogs or hedgerows or near water. Like many other European species, an individual will always remain in the same location. They do not require a great deal of heat. They shelter in vole burrows or beneath piles of stones or roots, especially bushes. They are also good swimmers and can cross wide rivers and lakes. Prey is mainly small rodents, frogs and toads, plus nesting birds and lizards, notably the Viviparous Lizard which often occurs in the same sort of habitat and at similar cool latitudes. Hibernation is from October to April, dependent on the weather.

Length: Average 45 centimeters, maximum 60 centimeters, or 24 to 32 inches.

Viper, Vipera Ammodytes

This very poisonous snake inhabits Herzegovina, but may also be found in Bosnia. This snake is also known as the European nose horned vipers for the protuberance of skin that looks like a small horn. Locally, the name of the snake is Poskok. This snake is considered to be the most poisonous snake in Europe. Its venom is hemeotoxic and a bite from this snake requires immediate medical attention.

Tourist Safety Precautions:

Although venomous snakes use their venom to secure food, they also use it for self-defense. Human accidents occur when you don't see or hear the snake, when you step on them, or when you walk too close to them.

Follow these simple rules to reduce the chance of accidental snake-bite:

- Don't put your hands into dark places, such as rock crevices, heavy brush, or hollow logs, without first investigating.
- Don't step over a fallen tree. Step on the log and look to see if there is a snake resting on the other side.
- Don't walk through heavy brush or tall grass without looking down. Look where you are walking.
- Don't pick up any snake unless you are absolutely positive it is not venomous.
- Don't sleep next to brush, tall grass, large boulders, or trees. They provide hiding places for snakes. Place your sleeping bag in a clearing. Use mosquito netting tucked well under the bag. This netting should provide a good barrier.
- Don't pick up freshly killed snakes without first severing the head. The nervous system may still be active and a dead snake can deliver a bite.

Vegetation: edible, medicinal, and poisonous

There are numerous species of edible plants in Herzegovina and the collection of these plants provides a variety of quality tourism experiences. A diversity of delicious berries and fruits, herbs, and mushrooms can be found throughout all regions of the country. In addition, there are many plants that serve as excellent medicines and these have improved the health of the people for centuries. All of these plants are found naturally in the forests and fields of the country. Their economic value has resulted in the creation of extensive commercial farms. Their personal value is apparent in the many private gardens planted near houses.

Tourist precautions

The search and collection of mushrooms, herbs, and fruits are very popular activities in Herzegovina. For the tourist who wishes to participate in these activities, a few precautions will result in successfully collecting edible plants and avoiding poisonous ones. The most important precautions are as follows:

- Be certain you know the types of plants you are collecting. It is essential to accurately verify the plants in order to avoid poisonous plants.
- Know the time of the year for harvesting the plants. Each type of plant becomes ripe at a specific time of the year and therefore has its own distinct time for harvesting.

- Well qualified guides should be used to search and collect plants. These individuals will not only help the tourist select the correct plant, but will have knowledge regarding the most likely location for finding the plants. The qualified guides can provide successful collection experiences for the tourist.

Communications

Tourists in Herzegovina can connect with the rest of the world through mobile phones (GSM B&H and ERONET). Although the entire country is served by mobile phone technology, there are exceptions that the tourist should be aware of. The mountainous terrain prevents signals in certain deep valleys and, of course, mobile phones will not work in caves.

Medical services

A limited number of hospitals and clinics are located throughout the country. By example, medical facilities in the Mount Velež Region include a hospital in Mostar and clinics in the communities. Ambulance service is provided throughout the entire country, but long travel distances, road conditions, and traffic congestion can severely lengthen response times.

A First Aid Kit is intended to be used during minor emergencies, but if properly stocked, can help you to deal with serious emergencies until professional medical help arrives. Having the right supplies nearby during an emergency can make a big difference in your ability to promptly respond.

The First Aid Kit should be large enough for you to clearly see and find anything you need quickly. The location of the kit should always be the same so you can find it immediately, but out of the reach of young children. Keep it apart from other medicines and supplies, and check it frequently to be sure to replace used and expired supplies. Add any special items, for example, an allergy kit that may be needed by you or your family.

The "Ten Essentials" for backcountry travel

In summary, if you seek a backcountry recreation experience, it is advisable to have a few essential items that will enhance your recreation experience and assist you in case of emergency. The outdoor recreation professionals have identified these items as the "Ten Essentials" and they are inexpensive and easy to obtain. These items include:

1. Map and compass
2. Flashlight
3. Whistle
4. Emergency shelter
5. Appropriate clothing

6. Sun protection
7. Waterproof matches or fire starter
8. Pocket knife
9. Water in container that can be re-filled
10. Personal First Aid Kit

APPENDIX: LANGUAGE

Pronunciation

Latin	Cyrillic	
A, a	А, а	as in party
B, b	Б, б	as in bed
C, c	Ц, ц	as in fats, bats
Č, č	Ч, ч	as in culture
Ć, ć	Ћ, ћ	as in cheese
D, d	Д, д	as in doctor
Dž, dž	Џ, џ	as in jam
Đ, đ	Ђ, ђ	as in jazz
E, e	Е, е	as in pet
F, f	Ф, ф	as in free
G, g	Г, г	as in goat
H, h	Х, х	as in hat
I, i	И, и	as in feet
J, j	Ј, ј	as in yet
K, k	К, к	as in kept
L, l	Л, л	as in leg
Lj, lj	Љ, љ	
M, m	М, м	as in mother
N, n	Н, н	as in no
Nj, nj	Њ, њ	as in new
O, o	О, о	as in hot
P, p	П, п	as in pie
R, r	Р, р	as in air
S, s	С, с	as in sand
Š, š	Ш, ш	as in shovel
T, t	Т, т	as in too
U, u	У, у	as in look
V, v	В, в	as in very
Z, z	З, з	as in zoo
Ž, ž	Ж, ж	as in treasure

Greetings

Good morning	*Dobro jutro*	Good afternoon	*Dobar dan*
Good evening	*Dobro veče*		
	[dobro veche]		
Good night	*Laku noć*	Hello/Goodbye	*Ćao* [chao]
What is your name?	*Kako se zoveš?*	How are you?	*Kako si?*
I am well	*Dobro sam*		

Basic phrases

please	*molim Vas*	thank you	*hvala*
you're welcome	*nema na čemu*		
	(reply to thank you)		
there is no	*nema*	excuse me	*oprostite*
give me	*dajte mi*	I like to	*želim*
I would like	*volio bih*	how?	*kako?*
how much?	*koliko?*	how much (cost)?	*koliko košta?*
what?	*šta?*	what's this ?	*šta je ovo?*
who?	*ko?*	when?	*kada?*
where?	*gdje?*	from where?	*odakle?*
where is	*gdje je*	do you know?	*znate li?*
I don't know	*ne znam*	I don't understand	*ne razumijem*
yes	*da*	no	*ne*
perhaps	*možda*	good	*dobro/dobra* (m/f)
how do you say?	*kako se kaže?*		

Numbers

one	*jedan*	nine	*devet*
two	*dva*	ten	*deset*
three	*tri*	eleven	*jedanaest*
four	*četiri*	sixteen	*šesnaest*
five	*pet*	twenty	*dvadeset*
six	*šest*	thirty one	*trideset i jedan*
seven	*sedam*	one hundred	*stotina*
eight	*osam*	one thousand	*hiljada/tisuća*

Food and drink

baked	*pečeno*	beef	*govedina*
beer	*pivo*	boiled	*kuhano*
bon appetite	*prijatno*	brandy	*loza*
bread	*hljeb/kruh*	breakfast	*doručak* [doruchak]
cabbage	*kupus*	cake	*kolač*
cheese	*sir*	coffee	*kafa/kava/kahva*
cucumber	*krastavac*	bean	*grah*
chicken	*piletina*	chips, french fries	*pomfrit*
dinner	*večera*	drink (noun)	*piće*
drink (verb)	*piti*	eggs	*jaja*
fish	*riba*	fried	*prženo*
fruit	*voće*	grilled	*sa roštilja*
home-made	*domaće*	juice	*đus*
lamb	*janjetina*	lemon	*limun*

lunch	*ručak*	meat	*meso*
milk	*mlijeko*	onion	*luk*
orange	*naranča*	pasta	*makaroni*
pears	*kruške*	peaches	*breskve*
plums	*šljive*	pork	*svinjetina*
potato	*krompir*	restaurant	*restoran*
rice	*riža*	salt	*so*
soup	*supa*	spirit	*rakija*
sugar	*šećer*	tomato	*paradajz*
tea	*čaj*	to eat	*jesti*
veal	*teletina*	vegetables	*povrće*
water	*voda*	wine	*vino*

Shopping

bank	*banka*	money	*novac*
bookshop	*knjižara*	postcard	*razglednica*
chemist	*apoteka*	post office	*pošta*
market	*pijaca*	shop	*prodavnica*

Getting around

bus	*autobus*	left/right	*lijevo/desno*
bus station	*autobusna stanica (autobusni kolodvor)*	straight on	*pravo*
train station	*željeznička stanica (željeznički kolodvor)*	ahead/behind	*naprijed/iza*
plane/airport	*avion/aerodrom (avion/zračna luka)*	up/down	*gore/dolje*
car/taxi	*auto/taksi*	under/over	*ispod/iznad*
petrol	*benzin*	north/south	*sjever/jug*
petrol station	*benzinska pumpa*	east/west	*istok/zapad*
entrance/exit	*ulaz/izlaz*	road/bridge	*put/most*
arrival/departure	*dolazak/polazak*	hill/mountain	*brdo/planina*
open/closed	*otvoreno/zatvoreno*	village/town	*selo/grad*
here/there	*ovdje/tamo*	waterfall	*vodopad*
near/far	*blizu/daleko*		

Time

hour/minute	*sat/minuta*	today/tomorrow	*danas/sutra*
week/day	*sedmica/dan (tjedan/dan)*	yesterday	*jučer*
year/month	*godina/mjesec*	morning	*jutro*
now	*sada*	afternoon	*poslijepodne*
soon	*uskoro*	evening/night	*večer/noć*
Monday	*ponedjeljak*	Friday	*petak*
Tuesday	*utorak*	Saturday	*subota*
Wednesday	*srijeda*	Sunday	*nedjelja*
Thursday	*četvrtak*	spring	*proljeće*
autumn	*jesen*	summer	*ljeto*
winter	*zima*		

Other useful words

a little	*malo*	a lot	*puno*
after	*poslije*	bathroom	*kupatilo*
bed	*krevet*	before	*prije*
block (of buildings)	*zgrade*	book	*knjiga*
car	*auto*	child	*dijete*
church	*crkva*	city	*grad*
cold	*hladno*	currency	*valuta*
dentist	*zubar*	doctor	*doktor*
dry	*suho*	embassy	*ambasada*
enough	*dosta*	fever	*temperatura*
film	*film*	hill	*brdo*
hospital	*bolnica*	hot	*toplo*
hotel	*hotel*	house	*kuća*
hut	*koliba*	ill	*bolestan*
key	*ključ*	lake	*jezero*
large	*veliko*	lorry	*kamion*
mosque	*džamija*	never	*nikad*
night	*noć*	nightclub	*disko*
nothing	*ništa*	police	*policija*
railway	*željeznica*	rain	*kiša*
river	*rijeka*	road	*put*
room	*soba*	sea	*more*
small	*malo*	street	*ulica*
to hurt	*boljeti*	to swim	*plivati*
toilet paper	*toalet papir*	too much	*previše*
tourist office	*turistički ured*	train	*voz/vlak*
village	*selo*	you	*Vi/ ti*

APPENDIX:
MORE INFORMATION

BOOKS

History/Politics

Simms, Brendan *Unfinest Hour; How Britain Helped to Destroy Bosnia* Penguin Press 2003

Malcolm, Noel *Bosnia, A short history* London Macmillan1994

Maas, Peter *Love Thy Neighbour* Papermac 1996

Lovrenović, Ivan *Bosnia, A Cultural History* Saqi Books 2001

Glenny, Misha *The Balkans 1804-1999, Nationalism, War and the Great Powers* Granta Books 2000 (second edition)

Holbrooke, Richard *To end a war* Modern Library 1998

Gutman, Roy *Witness to Genocide* Element Books 1993

Literature from Bosnia and Herzegovina (published in English)

Jergović, Miljenko *Sarajevo Marlboro* Consortium Book 2004

Selimović, Meša *Death of the Dervish* Northwestern University Press 1996

Andrić, Ivo *Bridge over the Drina* Harvill Press 1995

Hemon, Aleksandar *Question of Bruno* Picador 2001

Hemon, Aleksandar *Nowhere man* Picador 2003

WEBSITES

The web is being used more and more in Bosnia and Herzegovina these days. It is not, however, used on the scale as in the west. Most sites are, logically, in the local language, but there are quite a few good and helpful websites in English as well. Some of them simply offer a different angle as to what is going on in the country. When checking these sites you'll find some better than others but they all have some value for those looking to get to know Bosnia and Herzegovina a little bit better.

General

www.bosnia.org.uk - is the Bosnian Institute site that is a tremendous source of inside info and links to many local sites.

www.unsa.ba – University of Sarajevo gives a little insight as to what programs are available, what people are learning and what students in this part of the world are all about.

www.sarajevo-airport.ba – Flight schedules and other miscellaneous information about the coming and going to Sarajevo are available on this site.

www.imenik.telecom.ba – Online phone directory

www.rtvbih.ba – This is the official site of the Bosnia and Herzegovina National TV.

www.bhmac.org - is the official site of the Mine Action Center. It's not to scare you, it's meant to inform you.

Government

www.mvp.gov.ba – the Ministry of Foreign Affairs site gives an general overview of visa requirements and embassies here and abroad.

www.komorabih.com – this is the website of the Chambers of Foreign Commerce. The info provided is good and has many links to other informative sites in the country.

www.britishcouncil.ba - the British Council supports many cultural and educational activities. They are very up to date on the culture scene in BiH.

www.usis.com.ba – The American Embassy in BiH is very active. The site will give American citizens all the information they need while traveling as an American here.

www.ohr.int – The Office of the High Representative in BiH is the international governing body in the country. There are many updates on the economy, human rights, reform, and general info about who is who and what's going on in Bosnia and Herzegovina.

Tourism

www.bhtourism.ba – We made this site back in 2002. It's an OK site, but won't provide you with any information that is not already in this guide book series. There are plans to expand this site in the course of 2005.

www.sarajevo-tourism.com – Tourism Association of Sarajevo Canton is good site for general tourist information.

www.touristguide-ba.com – is a yellow pages 'tour guide' for the country. It does list an incredible amount of hotels, banks, restaurants, and even car repair garages. It may be of some help if you're looking for something in particular but the organization of it is not totally coherent.

www.sarajevo.ba - a site on the city of Sarajevo, what there is to see and what's happening in the fastest changing city in Europe.

www.city.ba - current events on cultural events in Sarajevo.

www.hercegovina.ba - a comprehensive web site on tourism in Herzegovina.

www.greenvisions.ba - an informative site on general information, eco-tourism, the environment and community development projects.

www.plivatourism.ba - an excellent site on eco-tourism in the Jajce area of central Bosnia.

www.veleztourism.ba - this site covers the cultural and natural heritage of the Blagaj and Mt. Velež area south of Mostar, including activities and accommodation.

Other interesting websites

Country history	http://vlib.iue.it/history/europe/Bosnia/
Country history	http://en.wikipedia.org/wiki/History of Bosnia and Herzegovina
Country history	http://www.kakarigi.net/manu/briefhis.htm
Historical maps	http://www.nytimes.com/specials/bosnia/context/ yugo1815.GIF.html
War history	http://www.friendsofbosnia.org/edu_bos.html
Towns and cities	http://www.fallingrain.com/world/BK/
Sarajevo	http://uvod.sarajevo.ba/
Banja Luka	http://www.banjaluka.rs.ba/_e/default.aspx
Mostar	http://en.wikipedia.org/wiki/Mostar
Tuzla	http://www.hr/tuzla/
Bihać	http://www.bihac.org/fotos/indexeng.html
Tourist guide	http://www.bosnie-herzegovina.net/e frames.html?/e toe.html
General info	http://www.bosnia-herzegowina.starttips.com/
Government	http://www.fbihvlada.gov.ba/#
Federation Gov.	http://www.fbihvlada.gov.ba/engleski/index.html
Rep. Srpska Gov.	http://www.vladars.net/en/
Canton Sarajevo	http://www.ks.gov.ba/eng/index.htm
Politics	http://en.wikipedia.org/wiki/Politics of Bosnia and Herzegovina

INDEX